The Naval War of 1914

The Naval War of 1914

Two Actions at Sea During the Early Phase
of the First World War

The Action off Heligoland

August 1914

L. Cecil Jane

Coronel and the Falkland Islands

A. Neville Hilditch

LEONAUR

The Naval War of 1914
Two Actions at Sea During the Early Phase of the First World War
The Action off Heligoland August 1914
by L. Cecil Jane
and
Coronel and the Falkland Islands
by A. Neville Hilditch

First published under the titles

The Action off Heligoland August 1914
and
Coronel and the Falkland Islands

Leonaur is an imprint of Oakpast Ltd

Copyright in this form © 2011 Oakpast Ltd

ISBN: 978-0-85706-539-1 (hardcover)
ISBN:978-0-85706-540-7 (softcover)

http://www.leonaur.com

Publisher's Notes

Contents

The Action off Heligoland August 1914

L. Cecil Jane

Contents

Introduction

Heligoland was originally a Danish possession; its population is mainly of Frisian extraction. From 1807 to 1890 it was held by Great Britain, having been seized for naval reasons, and was used as a naval station during the last stages of the Napoleonic War. In July 1890, by the Anglo-German agreement, concluded between Lord Salisbury and General von Caprivi, it was transferred to the German Empire.

The island lies in the North Sea, about 35 nautical miles NW. of Cuxhaven, 43 nautical miles N. of Wilhelmshaven, and 260 nautical miles E. by N. from Yarmouth. It consists of a rocky plateau, with an approximate area of 130 acres; a stretch of excellent sand to the south-eastward made it a favourite summer bathing resort for the people of Hamburg and north-eastern Germany. The island is peculiar in the fact that there is an entire absence of wheeled traffic.

HARBOURS OF HELIGOLAND

The original, or inner, harbour of the island is some 400 yards long by 200 yards wide. A new, or outer, harbour is in process of completion; it is intended to be about 900 yards long by 600 yards wide. The harbour is entered from the east, There are also two havens. The North Haven lies to the NE. of the island, between it and the sand-bank, known as Olde Hoven Brunnen; it is impossible to proceed from this haven to the harbour. The South Haven is ESE. of the island, between it and the rock of Düne. To the north of this haven, between it and the North Haven, there is an anchorage for torpedo craft, prohibited to all

11

other vessels than those of the German Navy. This anchorage is about five cables by two cables in area, and has an average depth of 2½ fathoms.

NAVAL VALUE OF THE ISLAND

Since its cession, considerable attention has been devoted to the island by the German Admiralty. One of the most serious difficulties with which the German naval administration has had to contend is the fact that on the North Sea coast of the empire there is no really satisfactory port. Hamburg and Bremen lie far up the Rivers Elbe and Weser. The original naval base on the North Sea, Wilhelmshaven, where is an imperial dockyard, suffers from the fact that Jade Bay is extremely sandy; the harbour can only be kept open by means of constant dredging. The new base, Cuxhaven, opposite the junction of the Kaiser Wilhelm Canal with the Elbe, suffers, in a slightly lesser degree, from the same drawback.

Hence every effort has been made to utilize Heligoland. It has been converted into a base for torpedo craft and submarines, and two Zeppelin sheds, said to be of the 'disappearing' variety, have been constructed on the island. But the value of Heligoland is much reduced by the fact that it suffers in a peculiar degree from erosion, and can, indeed, only be preserved from destruction by artificial means and at a considerable annual cost. The shores of the island are carefully protected by deposits of cement, which are constantly washed away in westerly gales and require frequent renewal.

FORTIFICATIONS

Heligoland, as well as the whole North Sea coast of Germany, has been very carefully fortified. The forts are of the cupola type, built of concrete, and are defended by 11-inch guns; the statement that the guns are 12-inch seems to be unfounded. Theoretically, both the island and the whole coast should be impregnable; it is supposed that a single shot from one of these guns would suffice to sink any ship. It must, however, be remembered that the value of cupola forts has been somewhat discounted by the experiences of Namur and other places.

ANCHORAGE OF HELIGOLAND

To the east of the island, immediately beyond the 'prohibited' anchorage, is the rock of Dune. It is protected by *groynes*, but both its area and shape are subject to frequent changes; it is in reality little more than a sandbank, serving as the site for three beacons. Beyond it, eastward, there is an anchorage for large vessels, which is satisfactory in westerly winds. It is probable that this is the anchorage which is mentioned in the dispatches as having been 'examined' on September 14, and that it has been utilized as a station for light cruisers. It is commanded by the guns of Heligoland.

BIGHT OF HELIGOLAND

The Bight of Heligoland, the scene of the operations described in the dispatches, is to the NE. of the island, from which it is distant some seven miles. It forms a channel, with an approximate width of eighteen miles and an average depth of nine fathoms, between the shallows near Heligoland and the shoals off the Holstein coast. Through it lies the regular course for ships proceeding north-wards from the Elbe ports.

BRITISH SHIPS ENGAGED

The following are brief details of the British vessels, mentioned as having taken part in the operations.

The date signifies date of completion; D. displacement; C. complement; G. guns. The speed given is the best recent speed, unless otherwise stated.

(1) BATTLE CRUISERS

Lion (1912: Devonport). D. 26,350. C. 1,000. Sp. 31·7 kts. Guns: eight 13·5-inch; sixteen 4-inch.
Queen Mary (1913: Clydebank). D. 27,000. C. 1,000. Sp. 33. Guns: (as *Lion*).
New Zealand (1912: Fairfield). D. 18,750. C. 800. Sp. 25 (designed: her sister's best recent speed is 29·13). Guns: eight 12-inch; sixteen 4-inch.
Invincible (1908: Elswick). D. 17,250. C. 750. Sp. 28·6. Guns: (as *New Zealand*).

13

All these vessels possess three submerged tubes. Their armour is Krupp.

The cruisers mentioned are the *Bacchante, Cressy, Euryalus,* and *Hogue.* They were sisters. Displacement, 12,000 tons: complement, 700 (*Euryalus,* as flagship, 745). Guns: two 9-2-inch; twelve 6-inch; thirteen 12-pounders. Two submerged tubes. Armour, Krupp.

The *Bacchante* (1902) was built at Clydebank; *Cressy* (1901), Fairfield; *Euryalus* (1903) and *Hogue* (1902),Vickers.

Best recent speeds were: *Bacchante,* 19-5 kts.; *Cressy,* 19-2; *Euryalus,* 20-3; *Hogue,* 17.

The *Hogue* and *Cressy,* with their sister, the *Aboukir,* were sunk by a German submarine on September 22.

(3) LIGHT CRUISERS

Arethusa (1913). D. 3,520. C. . Sp. (designed) 30 kts. Guns: two 6-inch; six 4-inch. Four tubes, above water. (Chatham.)

Lowestoft (1914). D. 5,400. C. . Sp. (designed) 24-75. Guns: nine 6-inch; four 3-pounders. Two submerged tubes. (Chatham.)

Liverpool (1910). D.. 4,800. C. 376. Sp. (designed) 25. Guns: two 6-inch; ten 4-inch; four 3-pounders. Two submerged tubes. Armour, Krupp. (Vickers.)

Fearless (1913). D. 3,440. C. 320. Sp. (designed) 25. Guns: ten 4-inch; four 3-pounders. Two tubes above water. Unarmoured. (Pembroke.)

Amethyst (1904). D. 3,000. C. 296. Sp. 20. Guns: twelve 4-inch; eight 3-pounders. Two tubes above water. (Elswick.)

(4) DESTROYERS

The destroyers mentioned were:

(a) Four of the L Class: D. 807 tons. Sp. 35. Armament: three 4-inch; four tubes. (1912-13.) The *Laurel* and *Liberty* are White boats; *Laertes,* Swan, Hunter & Richardson; *Laforey,* Fairfield.

14

(b) Two special boats of I Class, *Lurcher* and *Firedrake*. D. 790. C. 72. Sp. (designed) 32. Armament: two 4-inch; two 12-pounders; two tubes. (1911.) (Yarrow.)

(c) Three boats. Admiralty design, I Class: *Defender, Goshawk*, and *Ferret*. D. (nominal) 750. C. 72. Armament, as *Lurcher*. Sp. (designed) 27. (1911.) *Defender* is a Denny boat; *Ferret*, White; *Goshawk*, Beardmore. The actual displacement varies slightly from the nominal; speed in some cases rather above designed speed.

(5) SPECIAL SERVICE

Maidstone (1911: Scott's S. and E. Co.). Submarine depot ship. D. 3,600 tons. Sp. 14 kts.

(6) SUBMARINES

(a) D Class. Nos. 1, 2 and 8. D 1 (1907). D. 550-600. Maximum speed, 16-9. Tubes, 3. D 2 and D 8 (1910-11). D. 550-600. Maximum speed, 16-10. Tubes, 3.

(b) E Class. Nos. 4 to 9. (1912.) D. 725-810. Sp. 16-10. Tubes, 4.

Of the German vessels mentioned:

(1) Mainz (1909) (Vulkan Co.). D. 4,350. C. 362. Sp. (designed) 25-5. Guns: twelve 4-inch; four 5-pounders; four machine. Two submerged tubes. One of *Kolberg* class.

(2) Hela (1896: refitted, 1910), (Weser, Bremen). D. 2,040. C. 178. Guns: four 15½-pounders; six 6-pounders; two machine. One submerged tube; two above water. Sp. 18. Was to be replaced.

(3) V 187 (1909-11) (Vulkan). C. 82. Sp. 32-5. D. *circa* 650 tons. Armament: two 24-pounders; three tubes.

(4) S 126 (1906). D. 487. Sp. 28. C. 68. Armament: three 4-pounders; two machine. Three tubes.

The four-funnelled cruiser mentioned must have been either one of the *Breslau* and *Karlsrühe* class, or one of the *Roon* class. The former class comprises twelve vessels, four of the *Breslau* type, and eight of the *Karlsrühe* type (of which two were completed in 1913, two were due to be completed in the present year, two in 1915, and two later). Details of the *Breslau* class are as follows: D. 4,550. C. 370. Sp. (designed) 25½ kts. Guns: twelve 4-1-inch. Two submerged tubes. (The actual speed of these ships is above the designed speed.) Details of the *Karlsrühe* class are as follows: D. 4,900. C. 373. Sp. (designed) 28 kts. Guns: twelve 4-1-inch. Two submerged tubes. (1912-13.) The *Roon* class, containing two vessels, the *Roon* and *Yorck* (the latter since sunk), have: D. 9,050. C. 657. Sp. (designed) 21 kts. Guns: four 8-2-inch; ten 6-inch; eleven 24-pounders; four machine. Four submerged tubes. (1905-6.)

PAST SERVICES OF BRITISH OFFICERS

Some of the British officers concerned had already seen active service and gained distinctions.

Vice-Admiral (Acting) Sir David Beatty served as a lieutenant on the river Nile, during the operations of 1898, and conducted the bombardment of the Dongola forts. He also served as commander of the *Barfleur* at Tientsin in 1900.

Rear-Admiral Arthur H. Christian served on the expedition against King Kobo of Nimby, 1895, and captured M'weli, the stronghold of the Arab chief Mburuk in the same year.

Commodore Reginald Y. Tyrwhitt commanded the landing party during the disturbances at Blue-fields, 1894, and was thanked by the inhabitants.

Commodore Roger J. B. Keyes served against the Sultan of Vitu, 1890. In the *Fame*, he cut out four Chinese destroyers, 1900, and was promoted for this service.

Captain William F. Blunt was present at the blockade of Zanzibar, 1888-9, and also served in Crete, 1897-8, and in China, 1900.

Commander Charles R. Samson served in Somali-land, 1902-4. He made the first flight from the deck of a British warship in 1912.

Naval Engagement off Heligoland

Admiralty, 21st October, 1914.

The following despatches have been received from Vice-Admiral (Acting) Sir David Beatty, K.C.B., M.V.O., D.S.O., H.M.S, *Lion*, Rear-Admiral Arthur H. Christian, M.V.O., H.M.S. *Euryalus*, Commodore Reginald Y. Tyrwhitt, Commodore (T.), H.M.S. *Arethusa*, and Commodore Roger J. B. Keyes, C.B., M.V.O., Commodore (S.), reporting the engagement off Heligoland on Friday, the 28th August.

A memorandum by the Director of the Air Department, Admiralty, is annexed.

H.M.S. *Lion*,
1st September, 1914.

Sir,—I have the honour to report that on Thursday, 27th August, at 5 a.m., I proceeded with the First Battle Cruiser Squadron and First light cruiser Squadron in company, to rendezvous with the Rear-Admiral, *Invincible*.

At 4 a.m., 28th August, the movements of the Flotillas commenced as previously arranged, the Battle Cruiser Squadron and light cruiser Squadron supporting. The Rear-Admiral, *Invincible*, with *New Zealand* and four destroyers having joined my flag, the squadron passed through the pre-arranged rendezvous.

At 8.10 a.m. I received a signal from the Commodore (T), informing me that the flotilla was in action with the enemy. This was presumably in the vicinity of their pre-arranged rendezvous. From this time until 11 a.m. I remained about the vicinity ready to support as necessary, intercepting various signals, which contained no information on which I could act.

SUBMARINE ATTACK

At 11 a.m. the squadron was attacked by three submarines. The attack was frustrated by rapid manoeuvring and the four destroyers were ordered to attack them. Shortly after 11 a.m., various signals having been received indicating that the Commodore (T) and Commodore (S) were both in need of assistance, I ordered the light cruiser Squadron to support the Torpedo Flotillas.

Later I received a signal from the Commodore (T), stating that he was being attacked by a large cruiser, and a further signal informing me that he was being hard pressed and asking for assistance. The Captain (D), First Flotilla, also signalled that he was in need of help.

INTERVENTION OF THE BATTLE CRUISERS

From the foregoing the situation appeared to me critical. The flotillas had advanced only ten miles since 8 a.m., and were only about twenty-five miles from two enemy bases on their flank and rear respectively. Commodore Goodenough had detached two of his light cruisers to assist some destroyers earlier in the day, and these had not yet rejoined. (They rejoined at 2.30 p.m.) As the reports indicated the presence of many enemy ships—one a large cruiser—I considered that his force might not be strong enough to deal with the situation sufficiently rapidly, so at 11.30 a.m. the battle cruisers turned to E.S.E., and worked up to full speed. It was evident that to be of any value the support must be overwhelming and carried out at the highest speed possible.

I had not lost sight of the risk of submarines, and possible sortie in force from the enemy's base, especially in view of the mist to the South-East.

Our high speed, however, made submarine attack difficult, and the smoothness of the sea made their detection comparatively easy. I considered that we were powerful enough to deal with any sortie except by a battle squadron, which was unlikely to come out in time, provided our stroke was sufficiently rapid.

THE *MAINZ* ATTACKED

At 12.15 p.m. *Fearless* and First Flotilla were sighted retiring West. At the same time the light cruiser Squadron was observed to be engaging an enemy ship ahead. They appeared to have her beat.

ENEMY CRUISER ENGAGED WITH THIRD FLOTILLA

I then steered N.E. to sounds of firing ahead, and at 12.30 p.m. sighted *Arethusa* and Third Flotilla retiring to the westward engaging a cruiser of the *Kolberg* class on our port bow. I steered to cut her off from Heligoland, and at 12.37 p.m. opened fire. At 12.42 the enemy turned to N.E., and we chased at 27 knots.

LION ENGAGED WITH AN ENEMY CRUISER

At 12.56 p.m. sighted and engaged a two-funnelled cruiser ahead. *Lion* fired two salvoes at her, which took effect, and she disappeared into the mist, burning furiously and in a sinking condition. In view of the mist and that she was steering at high speed at right angles to *Lion*, who was herself steaming at 28 knots, the *Lion's* firing was very creditable.

Our destroyers had reported the presence of floating mines to the eastward and I considered it inadvisable to pursue her. It was also essential that the squadrons should remain concentrated, and I accordingly ordered a withdrawal. The battle cruisers turned north and circled to port to complete the destruction of the vessel first engaged.

SINKING OF THE *MAINZ*

She was sighted again at 1.25 p.m. steaming S.E. with colours still flying. *Lion* opened fire with two turrets, and at

British
Battle Cruiser
Squadron

N

W —— E

S

British
1st Light Cruiser
Squadron

3rd

British   ⊂ Arethusa

Destroyer

Flotilla   ⊂ Fearless

1st

British
7th Cruiser
Squadron

British Submarine
Flotilla

Heligoland

German Destroyers

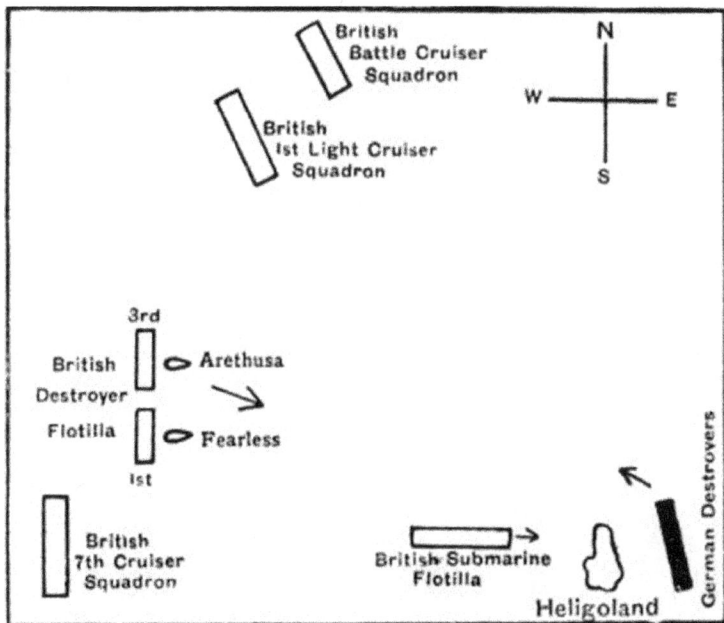

THE BATTLE OF HELIGOLAND BIGHT

The Battle of Heligoland Bight

1.35 p.m., after receiving two salvoes, she sank.

The four attached destroyers were sent to pick up survivors, but I deeply regret that they subsequently reported that they searched the area but found none.

SUBMARINE ATTACK ON *QUEEN MARY*

At 1.40 p.m. the battle cruisers turned to the northward, and *Queen Mary* was again attacked by a submarine. The attack was avoided by the use of the helm. *Lowestoft* was also unsuccessfully attacked. The battle cruisers covered the retirement until nightfall. By 6 p.m., the retirement having been well executed and all destroyers accounted for, I altered course, spread the light cruisers, and swept northwards in accordance with the commander-in-chief's orders. At 7.45 p.m. I detached *Liverpool* to Rosyth with German prisoners, 7 officers and 79 men, survivors from *Mainz*. No further incident occurred.—I have the honour to be. Sir, your obedient Servant,

(Signed) David Beatty,

Vice-Admiral.

The Secretary of the Admiralty.

WORK OF THE CRUISER FORCE

Euryalus,

28th September, 1914.

Sir,—I have the honour to report that in accordance with your orders a reconnaissance in force was carried out in the Heligoland Bight on the 28th August, with the object of attacking the enemy's light cruisers and destroyers.

The forces under my orders (*viz.*, the Cruiser Force, under Rear-Admiral H. H. Campbell, C.V.O., *Euryalus, Amethyst*, First and Third Destroyer Flotillas and the submarines) took up the positions assigned to them on the evening of the 27th August, and, in accordance with directions given, proceeded during the night to approach the Heligoland Bight.

The Cruiser Force under Rear-Admiral Campbell, with *Euryalus* (my flagship) and *Amethyst*, was stationed to intercept any enemy vessels chased to the westward. At 4.30 p.m. on the 28th August these Cruisers, having proceeded to the eastward, fell in with *Lurcher* and three other destroyers, and the wounded and prisoners in these vessels were transferred in boats to *Bacchante* and *Cressy*, which left for the Nore. *Amethyst* took *Laurel* in tow, and at 9.30 p.m. *Hogue* was detached to take *Arethusa* in tow. This latter is referred to in Commodore R. Y. Tyrwhitt's report, and I quite concur in his remarks as to the skill and rapidity with which this was done in the dark with no lights permissible.

INDIVIDUAL SERVICES MENTIONED

Commodore Reginald Y. Tyrwhitt was in command of the Destroyer Flotillas, and his report is enclosed herewith. His attack was delivered with great skill and gallantry, and he was most ably seconded by Captain William F. Blunt, in *Fearless*, and the officers in command of the destroyers, who handled their vessels in a manner worthy of the best traditions of the British Navy.

Commodore Roger J. B. Keyes, in *Lurcher*, had, on the 27th August, escorted some submarines into positions allotted to them in the immediate vicinity of the enemy's coast. On the morning of the 28th August, in company with *Firedrake*, he searched the area to the southward of the battle cruisers for the enemy's submarines, and subsequently, having been detached, was present at the sinking of the German Cruiser *Mainz*, when he gallantly proceeded alongside her and rescued 220 of her crew, many of whom were wounded. Subsequently he escorted *Laurel* and *Liberty* out of action, and kept them company till Rear-Admiral Campbell's Cruisers were sighted.

As regards the submarine officers, I would specially men-

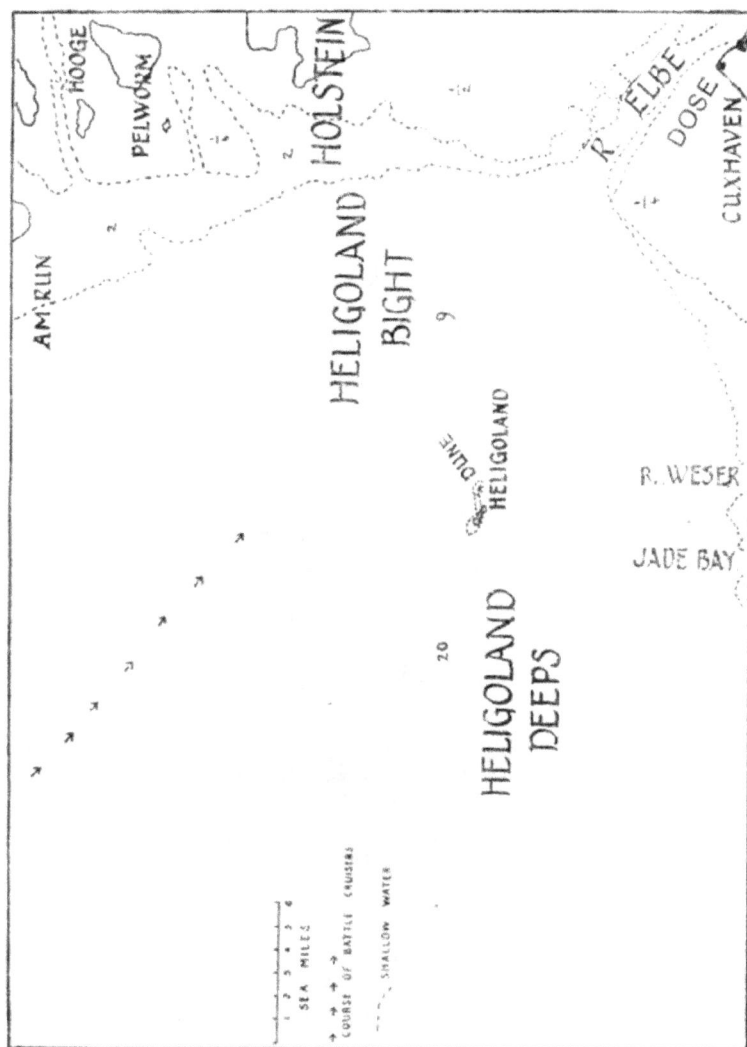

HELIGOLAND AND
THE COAST

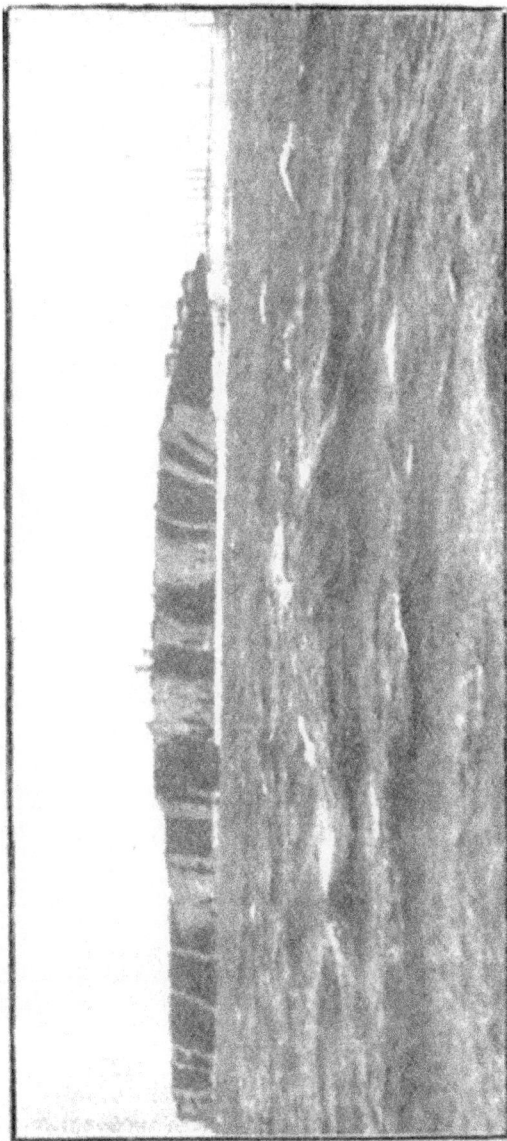

THE ISLAND OF HELIGOLAND

tion the names of:—

(a) Lieutenant-Commander Ernest W. Leir. His coolness and resource in rescuing the crews of the *Goshawk's* and *Defender's* boats at a critical time of the action were admirable.

(b) Lieutenant-Commander Cecil P. Talbot. In my opinion, the bravery and resource of the officers in command of submarines since the war commenced are worthy of the highest commendation.

I have the honour to be, Sir,

Your obedient Servant,

A. H. Christian,

Rear-Admiral.

The Secretary, Admiralty.

WORK OF DESTROYER FLOTILLA

H.M.S. *Lowestoft*,

26th September, 1914.

Sir,—I have the honour to report that at 5 a.m. on Thursday, 27th August, in accordance with orders received from Their Lordships, I sailed in *Arethusa*, in company with the First and Third Flotillas, except *Hornet*, *Tigress*, *Hydra*, and *Loyal*, to carry out the prearranged operations. H.M.S. *Fearless* joined the Flotillas at sea that afternoon.

At 6.53 a.m. on Friday, 28th August, an enemy's destroyer was sighted, and was chased by the 4th Division of the Third Flotilla.

From 7.20 to 7.57 a.m. *Arethusa* and the Third Flotilla were engaged with numerous destroyers and torpedo boats which were making for Heligoland; course was altered to port to cut them off.

ENEMY CRUISERS ENGAGED

Two cruisers, with 4 and 2 funnels respectively, were sighted on the port bow at 7.57 a.m., the nearest of which was engaged. *Arethusa* received a heavy fire from both cruisers

27

and several destroyers until 8. 15 a.m., when the four-funnelled cruiser transferred her fire to *Fearless*.

Close action was continued with the two-funnelled cruiser on converging courses until 8.25 a.m., when a 6-inch projectile from *Arethusa* wrecked the fore bridge of the enemy, who at once turned away in the direction of Heligoland, which was sighted slightly on the starboard bow at about the same time.

All ships were at once ordered to turn to the westward, and shortly afterwards speed was reduced to 20 knots.

DAMAGE DONE TO THE *ARETHUSA*

During this action *Arethusa* had been hit many times, and was considerably damaged; only one 6-inch gun remained in action, all other guns and torpedo tubes having been temporarily disabled.

Lieutenant Eric W. P. Westmacott (Signal Officer) was killed at my side during this action. I cannot refrain from adding that he carried out his duties calmly and collectedly, and was of the greatest assistance to me.

A fire occurred opposite No. 2 gun port side caused by a shell exploding some ammunition, resulting in a terrific blaze for a short period and leaving the deck burning. This was very promptly dealt with and extinguished by Chief Petty Officer Frederick W. Wrench, O.N. 158630.

The flotillas were re-formed in divisions and proceeded at 20 knots. It was now noticed that *Arethusa's* speed had been reduced.

SINKING OF AN ENEMY DESTROYER

Fearless reported that the 3rd and 5th Divisions of the First Flotilla had sunk the German Commodore's destroyer and that two boats' crews belonging to *Defender* had been left behind as our destroyers had been fired upon by a German Cruiser during their act of mercy in saving the survivors of the German Destroyer.

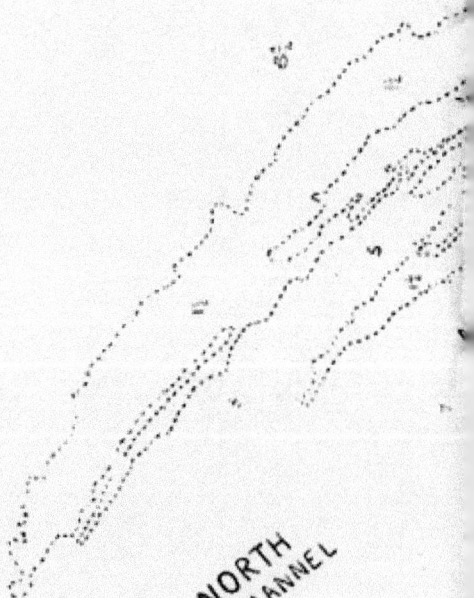

HELIGOLAND
BIGHT

9

9

7

6½

3

8

5

NORTH
CHANNEL

12

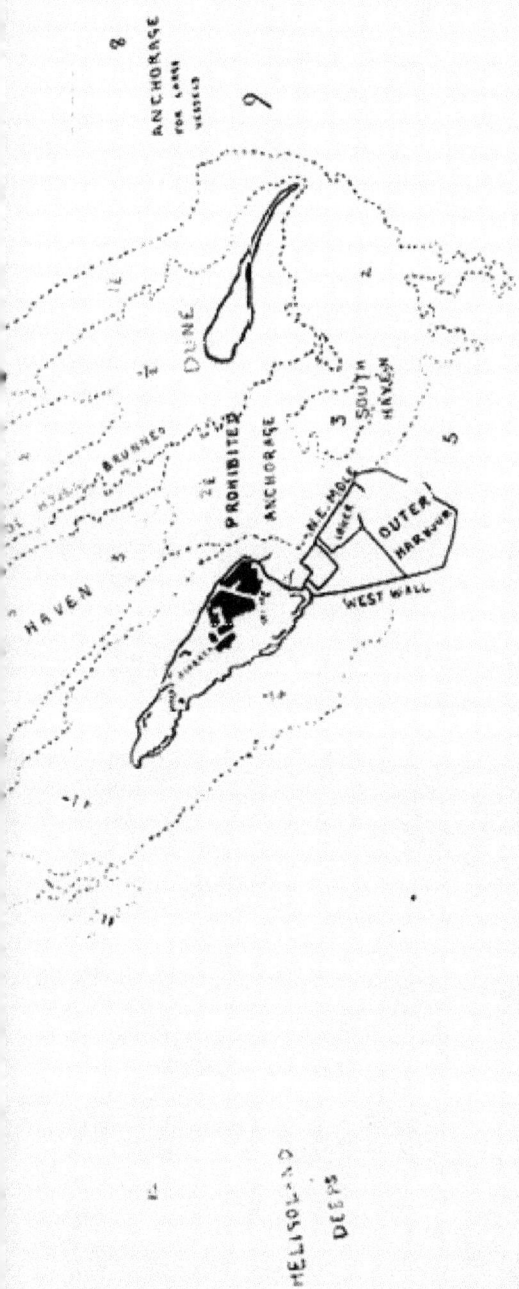

CHART OF HELIGOLAND

ANCHORAGE
FOR LARGE
VESSELS

8

9

DUNE

14

1¼

BRUNNEN

PROHIBITED
ANCHORAGE

2¼

HAVEN

SOUTH
HAVEN

3

2

5

1¼

NE MOLE

OUTER
HARBOUR

WEST WALL

6

SOUTH
CHANNEL

15

HELIGOLAND
DEEPS

HELIGOLAND

2¼

10 CABLES
ONE SEA MILE

At 10 a.m., hearing that Commodore (S) in *Lurcher* and *Firedrake* were being chased by light cruisers, I proceeded to his assistance with *Fearless* and the First Flotilla until 10.37 a.m., when, having received no news and being in the vicinity of Heligoland, I ordered the ships in company to turn to the westward.

All guns except two 4-inch were again in working order, and the upper deck supply of ammunition was replenished.

At 10.55 a.m. a four-funnelled German Cruiser was sighted, and opened a very heavy fire at about 11 o'clock.

Our position being somewhat critical, I ordered *Fearless* to attack, and the First Flotilla to attack with torpedoes, which they proceeded to do with great spirit. The cruiser at once turned away, disappeared in the haze and evaded the attack.

About 10 minutes later the same cruiser appeared on our starboard quarter. Opened fire on her with both 6-inch guns; *Fearless* also engaged her, and one division of destroyers attacked her with torpedoes without success.

The state of affairs and our position was then reported to the Admiral Commanding Battle Cruiser Squadron.

We received a very severe and almost accurate fire from this cruiser; salvo after salvo was falling between 10 and 30 yards short, but not a single shell struck; two torpedoes were also fired at us, being well directed, but short.

The cruiser was badly damaged by *Arethusa's* 6-inch guns and a splendidly directed fire from *Fearless*, and she shortly afterwards turned away in the direction of Heligoland.

SINKING OF THE *MAINZ*

Proceeded, and four minutes later sighted the three-funnelled cruiser *Mainz*. She endured a heavy fire from *Arethusa* and *Fearless* and many destroyers. After an action of approximately 25 minutes she was seen to be sinking by the head, her engines stopped, besides being on fire.

At this moment the light cruiser squadron appeared, and they very speedily reduced the *Mainz* to a condition which must have been indescribable.

I then recalled *Fearless* and the destroyers, and ordered cease fire.

We then exchanged broadsides with a large, four-funnelled cruiser on the starboard quarter at long range, without visible effect.

The Battle Cruiser Squadron now arrived, and I pointed out this cruiser to the Admiral Commanding, and was shortly afterwards informed by him that the cruiser in question had been sunk and another set on fire.

STATE OF THE WEATHER

The weather during the day was fine, sea calm, but visibility poor, not more than 3 miles at any time when the various actions were taking place, and was such that ranging and spotting were rendered difficult.

WITHDRAWAL OF THE FLOTILLA

I then proceeded with 14 destroyers of the Third Flotilla and 9 of the First Flotilla.

Arethusa's speed was about 6 knots until 7 p.m., when it was impossible to proceed any further, and fires were drawn in all boilers except two, and assistance called for.

At 9.30 p.m. Captain Wilmot S. Nicholson, of the *Hogue*, took my ship in tow in a most seamanlike manner, and, observing that the night was pitch dark and the only lights showing were two small hand lanterns, I consider his action was one which deserves special notice from Their Lordships.

I would also specially recommend Lieutenant-Commander Arthur P. N. Thorowgood, of *Arethusa*, for the able manner he prepared the ship for being towed in the dark. H.M. Ship under my command was then towed to the Nore, arriving at 5 p.m. on the 29th August. Steam was

SINKING OF THE *MAINZ*

The Sinking of Aboukir, Hogue and Cressy

H.M.S. *ARETHUSA*

THE BATTLE CRUISER LION

then available for slow speed, and the ship was able to proceed to Chatham under her own steam.

I beg again to call attention to the services rendered by Captain W. F. Blunt, of H.M.S. *Fearless*, and the commanding officers of the destroyers of the First and Third Flotillas, whose gallant attacks on the German Cruisers at critical moments undoubtedly saved *Arethusa* from more severe punishment and possible capture.

I cannot adequately express my satisfaction and pride at the spirit and ardour of my officers and Ship's Company, who carried out their orders with the greatest alacrity under the most trying conditions, especially in view of the fact that the ship, newly built, had not been 48 hours out of the dockyard before she was in action.

It is difficult to specially pick out individuals, but the following came under my special observation:—

H.M.S. *ARETHUSA*.

Lieutenant-Commander Arthur P. N. Thorowgood, First Lieutenant, and in charge of the After Control.

Lieutenant-Commander Ernest K. Arbuthnot (G.), in charge of the Fore Control.

Sub-Lieutenant Clive A. Robinson, who worked the range-finder throughout the entire action with extraordinary coolness.

Assistant Paymaster Kenneth E. Badcock, my Secretary, who attended me on the bridge throughout the entire action.

Mr. James D. Godfrey, Gunner (T), who was in charge of the torpedo tubes.

The following men were specially noted:—

Armourer Arthur F. Hayes, O.N. 342026 (Ch.).

Second Sick Berth Steward George Trolley, O.N. M.296 (Ch.).

Chief Yeoman of Signals Albert Fox, O.N. 194656 (Po.), on fore bridge during entire action.

Chief Petty Officer Frederick W. Wrench, O.N. 158630 (Ch.) (for ready resource in extinguishing fire caused by explosion of cordite).

Private Thomas Millington, R. M.L.I. , No. Ch. 17417.

Private William J. Beirne, R.M.L.I., No. Ch. 13540.

First Writer Albert W. Stone, O.N. 346080 (Po.).

I also beg to record the services rendered by the following officers and men of H.M. Ships under my orders:—

H.M.S. FEARLESS.

Mr. Robert M. Taylor, Gunner, for coolness in action under heavy fire.

The following Officers also displayed great resource and energy in effecting repairs to *Fearless* after her return to harbour, and they were ably seconded by the whole of their staffs:—

Engineer Lieutenant-Commander Charles de F. Messervy.

Mr. William Morrissey, Carpenter.

H.M.S. GOSHAWK.

Commander The Hon. Herbert Meade, who took his division into action with great coolness and nerve, and was instrumental in sinking the German Destroyer 'V.187', and, with the boats of his division, saved the survivors in a most chivalrous manner.

H.M.S. FERRET.

Commander Geoffrey Mackworth, who, with his division, most gallantly seconded Commander Meade of *Goshawk*.

H.M.S. LAERTES.

Lieutenant-Commander Malcolm L. Goldsmith, whose ship was seriously damaged, taken in tow, and towed out of action by *Fearless*.

Engineer Lieutenant-Commander Alexander Hill, for repairing steering gear and engines under fire.

Sub-Lieutenant George H. Faulkner, who continued to fight his gun after being wounded.

Mr. Charles Powell, Acting Boatswain, O.N. 209388, who was gunlayer of the centre gun, which made many hits. He behaved very coolly, and set a good example when getting in tow and clearing away the wreckage after the action.

Edward Naylor, Petty Officer, Torpedo Gunner's Mate, O.N. 189136, who fired a torpedo which the Commanding Officer of *Laertes* reports undoubtedly hit the *Mainz*, and so helped materially to put her out of action.

Stephen Pritchard, Stoker Petty Officer, O.N. 285152, who very gallantly dived into the cabin flat immediately after a shell had exploded there, and worked a fire hose.

Frederick Pierce, Stoker Petty Officer, O.N. 307943, who was on watch in the engine room and behaved with conspicuous coolness and resource when a shell exploded in No. 2 boiler.

H.M.S. *LAUREL*.

Commander Frank F. Rose, who most ably commanded his vessel throughout the early part of the action, and after having been wounded in both legs, remained on the bridge until 6 p.m., displaying great devotion to duty.

Lieutenant Charles R. Peploe, First Lieutenant, who took command after Commander Rose was wounded, and continued the action till its close, bringing his Destroyer out in an able and gallant manner under most trying conditions.

Engineer Lieutenant-Commander Edward H. T. Meeson, who be hatred with great coolness during the action, and steamed the ship out of action, although she had been very severely damaged by explosion of her own lyddite, by which the after funnel was nearly demolished. He subsequently assisted to carry out repairs to the vessel.

Sam Palmer, Leading Seaman (G.L. 2) O.N. 179529, who continued to fight his gun until the end of the action, although severely wounded in the leg.

Albert Edmund Sellens, Able Seaman (L.T.O.), O.N. 217245, who was stationed at the fore torpedo tubes; he remained at his post throughout the entire action, although wounded in the arm, and then rendered first aid in a very able manner before being attended to himself.

George H. Sturdy, Chief Stoker, O.N. 285547, and Alfred Britton, Stoker Petty Officer, O.N. 289893, who both showed great coolness in putting out a fire near the centre gun after an explosion had occurred there; several lyddite shells were lying in the immediate vicinity.

William R. Boiston, Engine Room Artificer, 3rd class, O.N. M. 1369, who showed great ability and coolness in taking charge of the after boiler room during the action, when an explosion blew in the after funnel and a shell carried away pipes and seriously damaged the main steam pipe.

William H. Gorst, Stoker Petty Officer, O.N.305616.

Edward Crane, Stoker Petty Officer, O.N. 307275.

Harry Wilfred Hawkes, Stoker 1st class, O.N. K. 12086.

John W. Bateman, Stoker 1st class, O.N. K. 12100.

These men were stationed in the after boiler room and conducted themselves with great coolness during the action, when an explosion blew in the after funnel, and shell carried away pipes and seriously damaged the main steam pipe.

H.M.S. *LIBERTY*.

The late Lieutenant-Commander Nigel K. W. Barttelot commanded the Liberty with great skill and gallantry throughout the action. He was a most promising and

COMMODORE REGINALD YORKE TYRWHITT

VICE-ADMIRAL DAVID BEATTY

able Officer, and I consider his death is a great loss to the Navy.

Engineer Lieutenant-Commander Frank A. Butler, who showed much resource in effecting repairs during the action.

Lieutenant Henry E. Horan, First Lieutenant, who took command after the death of Lieutenant-Commander Barttelot, and brought his ship out of action in an extremely able and gallant manner under most trying conditions.

Mr. Harry Morgan, Gunner (T), who carried out his duties with exceptional coolness under fire.

Chief Petty Officer James Samuel Beadle, O.N. 171735, who remained at his post at the wheel for over an hour after being wounded in the kidneys.

John Galvin, Stoker Petty Officer, O.N. 279946, who took entire charge, under the Engineer Officer, of the party who stopped leaks, and accomplished his task although working up to his chest in water.

H.M.S. LAFOREY

Mr. Ernest Roper, Chief Gunner, who carried out his duties with exceptional coolness under fire.

I have the honour to be. Sir,
Your obedient Servant,
R. Y. Tyrwhitt,
Commodore (T).

WORK OF SUBMARINES SINCE THE OUTBREAK OF WAR

H.M.S. Maidstone,
17th October, 1914.

Sir,—In compliance with Their Lordships' directions, I have the honour to report as follows upon the services performed by Submarines since the commencement of hostilities:—

RECONNAISSANCE IN HELIGOLAND BIGHT

Three hours after the outbreak of war, Submarines 'E.6'

(Lieutenant-Commander Cecil P. Talbot), and 'E.8' (Lieutenant-Commander Francis H. H. Good-hart), proceeded unaccompanied to carry out a reconnaissance in the Heligoland Bight. These two vessels returned with useful information, and had the privilege of being the pioneers on a service which is attended by some risk.

PROTECTION OF TRANSPORTS

During the transportation of the Expeditionary Force the *Lurcher* and *Firedrake* and all the submarines of the Eighth Submarine Flotilla occupied positions from which they could have attacked the High Sea Fleet, had it emerged to dispute the passage of our transports. This patrol was maintained day and night without relief, until the personnel of our Army had been transported and all chance of effective interference had disappeared.

OPERATIONS ON THE GERMAN COAST

These submarines have since been incessantly employed on the enemy's coast in the Heligoland Bight and elsewhere, and have obtained much valuable information regarding the composition and movement of his patrols. They have occupied his waters and reconnoitred his anchorages, and, while so engaged, have been subjected to skilful and well-executed anti-submarine tactics; hunted for hours at a time by torpedo craft and attacked by gunfire and torpedoes.

ENGAGEMENT OFF HELIGOLAND

At midnight on the 26th August, I embarked in the *Lurcher*, and, in company with *Firedrake* and Submarines 'D.2', 'D.8', 'E.4', 'E.5', 'E.6', 'E.7', 'E.8', and 'E.9' of the Eighth Submarine Flotilla, proceeded to take part in the operations in the Heligoland Bight arranged for the 28th August. The destroyers scouted for the submarines until nightfall on the 27th, when the latter proceeded independently to take up various positions from which they

46

could co-operate with the Destroyer Flotillas on the following morning.

At daylight on the 28th August the *Lurcher* and *Firedrake* searched the area, through which the battle cruisers were to advance, for hostile submarines, and then proceeded towards Heligoland in the wake of Submarines 'E.6', 'E.7', and 'E.8', which were exposing themselves with the object of inducing the enemy to chase them to the westward.

State of the Weather

On approaching Heligoland, the visibility, which had been very good to seaward, reduced to 5,000 to 6,000 yards, and this added considerably to the anxieties and responsibilities of the commanding officers of submarines, who handled their vessels with coolness and judgment in an area which was necessarily occupied by friends as well as foes.

Low visibility and calm sea are the most unfavourable conditions under which submarines can operate, and no opportunity occurred of closing with the enemy's cruisers to within torpedo range.

SINKING OF 'V.187'

Lieutenant-Commander Ernest W. Leir, Commanding Submarine 'E.4', witnessed the sinking of the German Torpedo Boat Destroyer 'V.187' through his periscope, and, observing a cruiser of the *Stettin* class close, and open fire on the British Destroyers which had lowered their boats to pick up the survivors, he proceeded to attack the cruiser, but she altered course before he could get within range. After covering the retirement of our destroyers, which had had to abandon their boats, he returned to the latter, and embarked a lieutenant and nine men of *Defender*, who had been left behind.

The boats also contained two officers and eight men of 'V.187', who were unwounded, and eighteen men who were badly wounded. As he could not embark the latter,

Lieutenant-Commander Leir left one of the officers and six unwounded men to navigate the British boats to Heligoland. Before leaving he saw that they were provided with water, biscuit, and a compass. One German officer and two men were made prisoners of war.

INDIVIDUAL SERVICES

Lieutenant-Commander Leir's action in remaining on the surface in the vicinity of the enemy and in a visibility which would have placed his vessel within easy gun range of an enemy appearing out of the mist, was altogether admirable.

This enterprising and gallant officer took part in the reconnaissance which supplied the information on which these operations were based, and I beg to submit his name, and that of Lieutenant-Commander Talbot, the commanding officer of 'E.6', who exercised patience, judgment and skill in a dangerous position, for the favourable consideration of Their Lordships.

SINKING OF THE *HELA*

On the 13th September, 'E.9' (Lieutenant-Commander Max K. Horton) torpedoed and sank the German light cruiser *Hela* six miles south of Heligoland.

A number of destroyers were evidently called to the scene after 'E.9' had delivered her attack, and these hunted her for several hours.

EXAMINATION OF THE HELIGOLAND ANCHORAGE

On the 14th September, in accordance with his orders, Lieutenant-Commander Horton examined the outer anchorage of Heligoland, a service attended by considerable risk.

On the 25th September, Submarine 'E.6' (Lieutenant-Commander C. P. Talbot), while diving, fouled the moorings of a mine laid by the enemy. On rising to the surface she weighed the mine and sinker; the former was securely fixed between the hydroplane and its guard; fortunately, however, the horns of the mine were pointed outboard. The weight of the sinker made it a difficult and dangerous matter to lift the mine clear without exploding it. After half an hour's patient work this was effected by Lieutenant Frederick A. P. Williams-Freeman and Able Seaman Ernest Randall Cremer, Official Number 214235, and the released mine descended to its original depth.

SINKING OF 'S.126'

On the 6th October, 'E.9' (Lieutenant-Commander Max K. Horton), when patrolling off the Ems, torpedoed and sank the enemy's destroyer, 'S.126.'

The enemy's Torpedo Craft pursue tactics which; in connection with their shallow draft, make them exceedingly difficult to attack with torpedo, and Lieutenant-Commander Horton's success was the result of much patient and skilful zeal. He is a most enterprising submarine officer, and I beg to submit his name for favourable consideration.

Lieutenant Charles M. S. Chapman, the second in command of 'E.9', is also deserving of credit.

DIFFICULTIES OF THE SUBMARINE WORK

Against an enemy whose capital vessels have never, and light cruisers have seldom, emerged from their fortified harbours, opportunities of delivering Submarine attacks have necessarily been few, and on one occasion only, prior to the 13th September, has one of our submarines been within torpedo range of a cruiser during daylight hours.

During the exceptionally heavy westerly gales which prevailed between the 14th and 21st September, the position of the submarines on a lee shore, within a few miles of the enemy's coast, was an unpleasant one.

The short steep seas which accompany westerly gales in the Heligoland Bight made it difficult to keep the conning tower hatches open. There was no rest to be obtained, and even when cruising at a depth of 60 feet, the submarines were rolling considerably, and pumping—*i.e.*, vertically moving about twenty feet.

I submit that it was creditable to the commanding officers that they should have maintained their stations under such conditions.

EAGERNESS TO SERVE IN THE BIGHT

Service in the Heligoland Bight is keenly sought after by the commanding officers of the Eighth Submarine Flotilla, and they have all shown daring and enterprise in the execution of their duties. These officers have unanimously expressed to me their admiration of the cool and gallant behaviour of the officers and men under their command. They are, however, of the opinion that it is impossible to single out individuals when all have performed their duties so admirably, and in this I concur.

SUBMARINES ENGAGED

The following Submarines have been in contact with the enemy during these operations:—

'D.1' (Lieutenant-Commander Archibald D. Cochrane).

'D.2' (Lieutenant-Commander Arthur G. Jameson).

'D.3' (Lieutenant-Commander Edward C. Boyle).

'D.5' (Lieutenant-Commander Godfrey Herbert).

'E.4' (Lieutenant-Commander Ernest W. Leir).
'E.5' (Lieutenant-Commander Charles S. Benning).

'E.6' (Lieutenant-Commander Cecil P. Talbot).

'E.7' (Lieutenant-Commander Ferdinand E. B. Feilmann).

'E.9' (Lieutenant-Commander Max K. Horton).

I have the honour to be, Sir,
Your obedient Servant,
(Signed) Roger Keyes,
Commodore S).

Commander Charles R. Samson, R.N., was in command of the Aeroplane and Armoured Motor Support of the Royal Naval Air Service (Naval Wing) at Dunkerque, between the dates 1st September to 5th October.

Aeroplane Skirmishes in September

During this period several notable air reconnaissances were made, and skirmishes took place. Of these particular mention may be made of the aeroplane attack on 4th September on 4 enemy cars and 40 men, on which occasion several bombs were dropped; and of the successful skirmishes at Cassel on 4th September, Savy on 12th September, Aniche on 22nd September, Orchies on 23rd September.

Attack on Düsseldorf (Sept. 22)

On the 22nd September, Flight Lieutenant C. H. Collet, of the Royal Naval Air Service (Naval Wing of the Royal Flying Corps), flying a Sopwith tractor biplane, made a long flight and a successful attack on the German Zeppelin Airship Shed at Düsseldorf.

Lieutenant Collet's feat is notable—gliding down from 6,000 feet, the last 1,500 feet in mist, he finally came in sight of the Airship Shed at a height of 400 feet, only a quarter of a mile away from it.

Attack on Düsseldorf (Oct. 8)

Flight Lieutenant Marix, acting under the orders of Squadron Commander Spenser Grey, carried out a successful attack on the Düsseldorf airship shed during the afternoon of the 8th October. From a height of 600 feet he dropped two bombs on the shed, and flames 500 feet high were seen within thirty seconds. The roof of the shed was also observed to collapse.

Lieutenant Marix's machine was under heavy fire from rifles and *mitrailleuse* and was five times hit whilst making the attack.

Squadron Commander Spenser Grey, whilst in charge of a flight of naval aeroplanes at Antwerp, penetrated during a 3¾ hours' flight into the enemy's country as far as Cologne on the 8th October. He circled the city under fire at 600 feet and discharged his bombs on the military railway station. Considerable damage was done.

11th October, 1914.

Coronel and the Falkland Islands

A. Neville Hilditch

Contents

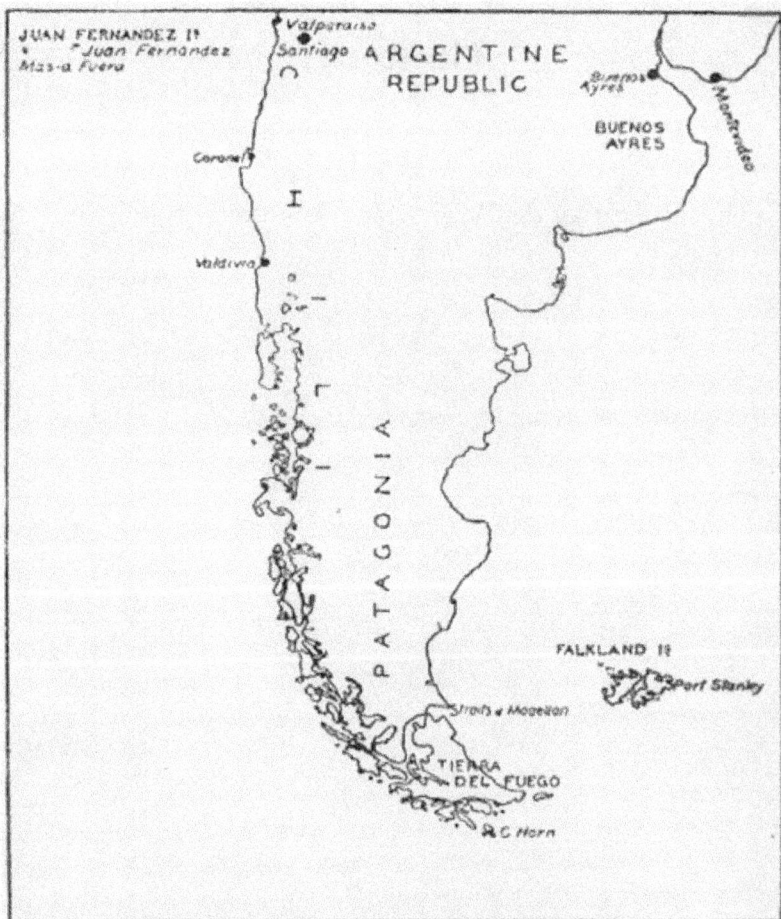

JUAN FERNANDEZ I?
* * Juan Fernandez
Mas-a Fuera

Valparaiso
Santiago

ARGENTINE
REPUBLIC

Buenos
Ayres

Montevideo

BUENOS
AYRES

Coronel

I

Valdivia

PATAGONIA

FALKLAND I?

Port Stanley

Straits of Magellan

TIERRA
DEL FUEGO

C. Horn

SOUTHERN SOUTH AMERICA

The Struggle for the Pacific Trade Routes

In 1592, John Davis, the arctic explorer, after whom the strait between Greenland and the North American mainland is named, made an attempt, in company with Thomas Cavendish, to find a new route to Asia by the Straits of Magellan. Differences arose between the two leaders. One was an explorer: the other had a tendency towards freebooting. They parted off the coast of Patagonia. Davis, driven out of his course by stormy weather, found himself among a cluster of unknown and uninhabited islands, some three hundred miles east of the Straits of Magellan. This group, after many changes and vicissitudes, passed finally into the hands of Great Britain, and became known as the Falkland Islands.

They consist of two large islands and of about one hundred islets, rocks, and sandbanks. The fragments of many wrecks testify to the dangers of navigation, though masses of giant seaweed act as buoys for many of the rocks. So numerous are the penguins, thronging in battalions the smaller islands and the inland lagoons, that the governor of the colony is nicknamed King of the Penguins. As New Zealand is said to be the most English of British possessions, the Falklands may perhaps be appropriately termed the most Scottish. Their general appearance resembles that of the Outer Hebrides. Of the population, who number some 2,000, a large proportion are of Scottish extraction. The climate is not unlike that of the north-west of Scotland. The winters are misty and rainy, but not excessively cold. So violent are the winds, that it is said to be impossible to play tennis or croquet, unless walls are erected as shelter, while cabbages grown in the kitchen-gardens of the shepherds, the only cultivated ground, are at times uprooted and scattered like straw.

The surface, much of which is bogland, is in some parts mountainous, and is generally wild and rugged. Small streams and shallow freshwater tarns abound. A natural curiosity, regarded with great wonder, exists in 'stone-rivers'; long, glistening lines of quartzite rock debris, which, without the aid of water, slide gradually to lower levels. There are no roads. Innumerable sheep, the familiar Cheviots and Southdowns, graze upon the wild scurvy-grass and sorrel. The colony is destitute of trees, and possesses but few shrubs. The one tree that it can boast, an object of much care and curiosity, stands in the Governor's garden. The seat of government, and the only town, is Port Stanley, with a population of about 950.

Its general aspect recalls a small town of the western highlands of Scotland. Many of the houses, square, white-washed, and grey-slated, possess small greenhouse-porches, gay with fuchsias and pelargoniums, in pleasing contrast to the prevailing barrenness. A small cathedral, Christ Church, and an imposing barracks, generally occupied by a company of marines, stand in the midst of the town. The Government House might be taken for an Orkney or Shetland manse. The administration of the colony and of its dependencies is vested in a Governor, aided by a Colonial Secretary, and by an executive and a legislative council. The Governor acts as Chief Justice, and the Colonial Secretary as Police Magistrate.

There is a local jail, capable of accommodating six offenders at a time. Its resources are not stated, however, to be habitually strained. Education is compulsory: the Government maintains schools and travelling teachers. The inhabitants are principally engaged in sheep-farming and seafaring industries. The colony is prosperous, with a trade that of late years has grown with extraordinary rapidity. The dividends paid by the Falkland Islands Company might excite the envy of many a London director.

Stanley's importance has been increased by the erection of wireless installation; and as a coaling and refitting station for vessels rounding the Horn, the harbour, large, safe, and accessible, is of immense value.

To this remote outpost of empire came tidings of war in August, 1914. Great excitement and enthusiasm prevailed. News was very slow in getting through: the mails, usually a month in transit, became very erratic. But the colony eagerly undertook a share in the burden of the Empire; £2,250 was voted towards the war-chest; £750 was collected on behalf of the Prince of Wales's Fund. Detached, though keen, interest changed, however, as the weeks passed, to intimate alarm. The Governor, Mr. Allardyce, received a wireless message from the Admiralty that he must expect a raid. German cruisers were suspected to be in the neighbourhood.

Never before had the colony known such bustle and such excitement. They, the inhabitants of the remote Falklands, were to play a part in the struggle that was tugging at the roots of the world's civilization. The exhilaration of expectancy and of danger broke suddenly into their uneventful, though not easy, lives. But there was cause for keen anxiety. The colonists were, however, reassured for a time by a visit from three British warships, the cruisers *Good Hope, Monmouth,* and *Glasgow,* with the armed liner *Otranto.*

The *Good Hope* had, at the declaration of war, been patrolling the Irish coast. She was ordered to sweep the Atlantic trade routes for hostile cruisers. She reached the coast of North America, after many false alarms, stopping English merchantmen on the way, and informing the astonished skippers of the war and of their course in consequence. When forty miles east of New York, Rear-Admiral Sir Christopher Cradock came aboard with his staff, and hoisted his flag. The Admiral turned southwards, sweeping constantly for the enemy. Passing through the West Indies, he proceeded to the coast of Brazil. Here he was joined by the *Glasgow.* The *Good Hope* had picked up the *Monmouth* previously.

The three ships, accompanied by the auxiliary cruiser *Otranto*, kept a southerly course. The discovery at Pernambuco of twenty-three German merchantmen snugly ensconced behind the breakwater, in neutral harbour, proved very galling. The Straits of Magellan and the cold Tierra del Fuego were at length reached. The squadron was on the scent of three German cruisers, the *Leipzig, Dresden*, and *Nürnberg*. It was suspected that they had gone to coal in this remote corner of the oceans. Their secret and friendly wireless stations were heard talking in code. The British made swoops upon wild and unsurveyed bays and inlets. The land around was covered with ice and snow, and the many huge glaciers formed a sight wonderful to behold. But the search had proved fruitless. After rounding the Horn several times, the squadron had turned towards the Falklands.

The inhabitants could not long rely, however, upon these powerful guardians. The squadron, after coaling, departed, again bound for the Straits of Magellan and the Pacific. Its strength was certainly adequate to tackle with success the three German ships believed to be in the vicinity. The colony could depend upon Admiral Cradock to protect it to the best of his ability. But it was not improbable that the enemy might evade the patrolling cruisers, and descend upon the hapless Falklands without warning. The Governor saw the advisability of instant preparation. On October 19 he issued a notice that all women and children were to leave Stanley. Provisions, stores, and clothes were hastily removed into the interior, which was locally termed the 'camp'.

The colony possessed a Volunteer Rifle Company, some 120 strong, and two nine-pounder field-guns. Further volunteers were enrolled and armed. Suddenly, on November 3, an alarming wireless message was received. The *Good Hope* and the *Monmouth* were reported to have been sunk off the coast of Chili. It was unsigned. There was no proof of its authenticity. But the next day another message followed from the captain of the *Glasgow*. The disaster was confirmed. The *Glasgow*, in company with H.M.S. *Canopus*, was running with all speed for the Falklands.

THE GERMAN CRUISER DRESDEN

They were probably being followed by the victorious Germans. Four days of acute suspense followed. The situation seemed critical. The Governor passed several nights without taking off his clothes, in expectancy of wireless messages that needed instant decoding. People slept beside their telephones. Early in the morning of Sunday, November 8, the two warships arrived.

The *Glasgow* was badly damaged. An enormous hole, three feet by nine feet, gaped in her side. A shell had wrecked Captain Luce's cabin, giving off fumes such as rendered unconscious several men who rushed in to put out the fire. The vessel had escaped any serious outbreak, however, and had suffered only four slight casualties. Warm tributes were paid by the captain to the cool and disciplined conduct of both officers and men. The *Canopus* had not been engaged. But a narrative of the preceding events may now be appropriate.

Vice-Admiral the Graf Maximilian von Spee was in command, at the outbreak of hostilities, of the German China fleet stationed at Tsing Tau. A successor, indeed, had been appointed, and was on the way to relieve him. But just before war was declared von Spee and his squadron steamed off into the open seas. To remain at Tsing Tau while vastly superior forces were closing in upon him would be to little purpose. Commerce raiding offered a field for rendering valuable service to the Fatherland. The *Emden* was dispatched to the southern seas. The *Leipzig* and the *Nürnberg* proceeded across the Pacific, and began to prey upon the western coast of South America.

Half the maritime trade of Chili was carried in English ships. Many of them might be seized and destroyed at little risk. The Admiral, with his two remaining vessels, the *Scharnhorst* and the *Gneisenau*, successfully evaded the hostile fleets for some time. On September 14 he touched at Apia, in German Samoa, familiar to readers of Robert Louis Stevenson. It could be remembered how, fifteen years before, this colony, shortly to fall before a New Zealand expeditionary force, had been a bone of contention between Great Britain and Germany. Captain Sturdee, whom von Spee was soon to meet in more arduous operations, had on that occasion commanded the British force in the tribal warfare.

Eight days later, on September 22, the two German cruisers arrived off Papeete, in Tahiti, one of the loveliest of Pacific islands. A small disarmed French gunboat lying there was sunk, and the town was bombarded. The Admiral, planning a concentration of German ships, then steamed east across the Pacific. He got into touch with friendly vessels. By skilful manoeuvring he finally brought five warships, with colliers, together near Valparaiso.

The German ships were all of recent construction. The *Scharnhorst* and the *Gneisenau* were armoured cruisers of 11,600 tons. The *Leipzig*, the *Nürnberg*, and the *Dresden* were light cruisers of about 3,500 tons. The armament of the larger vessels included eight 8-2-inch and six 6-inch guns. The smaller relied upon either ten or twelve 4-inch pieces. Each ship carried torpedo tubes, and the speed of each was about twenty-two or twenty-three knots an hour. The *Dresden*, however, could go to twenty-seven knots. The squadron possessed all-important allies. Several German merchant-marine companies, notably the Kosmos, plied along the Chilian coast. The tonnage of their vessels, indeed, amounted to no less than half that of the English companies.

The advance of German enterprise in Chili in recent years had been very marked. Von Spee's great stumbling-block was coal. The laws of war prevented him from sending more than three of his warships into a neutral port at the same time, from staying there more than twenty-four hours, from taking more coal than was necessary to reach the nearest German harbour, from coaling again for three months at a port of the same nationality. But if German merchantmen, hampered by no such restrictions, could constantly renew his supplies, the difficulty of fuel could be to some extent met. Provisions and secret information as to British movements could also be obtained through the same source. Such employment of merchantmen, however, being contrary to international law, would have to be clandestine.

The great Pacific coast offered numerous harbours and abundant facilities for being utilized as a base under such conditions. It showed many historic precedents for bold and adventurous exploits which could not fail to appeal to an admiral whose family, ennobled by the Emperor Charles VI, took pride in its ancient and aristocratic lineage. The occasion seemed opportune, moreover, for the accomplishment, by himself, his officers, and men, of deeds which should inspire their posterity as British naval traditions, for lack of other, at present inspired them. They could recall how, on this very coast, in 1578-9, Drake, the master raider, had seized a Spanish treasure-ship off Valdivia, had descended like a hawk upon Callao, had pounced upon another great galleon, taking nearly a million pounds in gold and silver; and how the intrepid mariner, sailing off into the unknown ocean, had circumnavigated the globe, while the furious de Toledo waited, with eleven warships, in the Straits of Magellan.

Why, indeed, should not the Germans imitate, in the twentieth century, the deeds of Drake in the sixteenth? If they preyed ruthlessly upon English merchantmen, laden with the wealth of the West, if they made a descent upon the Falkland Islands, if then they were to disappear into the wide Pacific, a career of splendid adventure and of unbounded usefulness would earn for them both the respect and the plaudits of the world. Australian and Japanese warships were sweeping the eastern Pacific for them. Many British vessels, called from useful employment elsewhere, would have to join in the search for them.

But so vast was the area that they might elude their enemies for months. British ships were already cruising near the Horn, possibly unaware that a concentration of the Germans had been effected. It was not unlikely that von Spee might be able to cut off and to destroy stray units of the patrolling squadrons. The Graf could see many opportunities of serving effectively the cause of the Fatherland. He must utilize them to the full. Sir Christopher Cradock, meanwhile, had rounded the Horn once more, and was cruising northwards up the coast of Chili. That coast, indeed, once the haunt of *corsairs* and filibusters, was rich in historic associations and in natural beauties.

An element of grandeur and of mystery seemed to hover around the countless ridges and peaks of the Andes, stretching, with the gleam of their eternal snows, for four thousand miles, and gazing down across the illimitable waters of the Occident. Upon the *plateaux*, miles above sea level, stood old stone temples and pyramids which rivalled in massiveness and ingenuity those of Egypt and of Babylon. The student of ancient civilizations could trace, in the mystic deities of the Incas and Araucanians, a strange similarity to the deities of the Chaldeans and Babylonians. Speculation upon this analogy formed a fascinating theme. This coast, too, was sacred to memories that could not but be dear to sailors as gallant and daring as Cradock, since his services in China, in 1900, was known to be.

Among other familiar British names, Cochrane, Lord Dundonald, had won enduring glory in the struggle for Chilian independence, nearly a hundred years before. The conditions of naval warfare had, indeed, through the introduction of armour and the perfection of weapons, radically changed since Cochrane, in a series of singularly audacious exploits, had overcome the fleets of Spain. Sea-fighting had become purely a matter of science. The object of strategy was to concentrate faster ships and more powerful guns against weaker force. The odds with which Cradock was to contend against the Germans were greater in proportion, if less in bulk, than the odds with which Cochrane had contended, with his peasant crews and his hulks, against the Spanish 'wooden-walls'.

Admiral Cradock now knew that there were two more cruisers in the neighbourhood than had at first been supposed. The *Canopus* had accordingly been sent to join his squadron. But she was a battleship, and much slower than the cruisers. She could travel no faster than at eighteen knots. Cradock proceeded northwards, ahead of the *Canopus*, made a rendezvous off Concepçion Bay for his colliers, and went into Coronel and on to Valparaiso to pick up news and receive letters. The squadron

H.M.S. *Good Hope*

then returned to the rendezvous and coaled. This completed, the Admiral directed the *Glasgow* to proceed again to Coronel to dispatch certain cables. Captain Luce duly carried out his mission, and left Coronel at nine o'clock on Sunday morning, November 1, steaming northwards to rejoin the other ships. A gale was rising. The wind was blowing strongly from the south. Heavy seas continually buffeted the vessel. At two o'clock a wireless signal was received from the *Good Hope*.

Apparently from wireless calls there was an enemy ship to northward. The squadron must spread out in line, proceeding in a direction north-east-by-east, the flag-ship forming one extremity, the *Glasgow* the other. It was to move at fifteen knots. At twenty minutes past four in the afternoon, smoke was observed upon the horizon. The *Glasgow* put on speed and approached. Officers soon made out the funnels of four cruisers. It was the enemy. The Germans, their big armoured cruisers leading, and the smaller behind, gave chase.

The *Glasgow* swept round to northward, calling to the flag-ship with her wireless. Von Spee, anticipating this move, at once set his wireless in operation, in order to jamb the British signals. Captain Luce soon picked up the *Monmouth* and the *Otranto*, and the three ships raced northwards towards the flagship, the *Glasgow* leading. At about five o'clock the *Good Hope* was seen approaching. The three ships wheeled into line behind her, and the whole squadron now proceeded south. Von Spee, coming up from that direction in line ahead, about twelve miles off, changed his course and also proceeded south, keeping nearer to the coast. The wind was now blowing almost with the force of a hurricane.

So heavy was the sea that small boats would have been unable to keep afloat. But the sky was not completely overcast, and the sun was shining. Firing had not opened. The washing of the seas and the roaring of the wind deafened the ear to other sounds. The warship of today, when her great turbines are whirling round at their highest speed, moves without throb and almost without vibration through the waves. The two squadrons, drawing level, the Germans nearer to the coast, raced in the teeth of the gale, in two parallel lines, to the south.

Sir Christopher Cradock could not but realize that the situation was hazardous. He had three vessels capable of fighting men-of-war. The *Otranto* was only an armed liner, and must withdraw when the battle developed. The *Good Hope* displaced some 14,000 tons, and was armed with two 9-2-inch and sixteen 6-inch guns. The *Monmouth*, with a tonnage of 9,800, carried fourteen 6-inch pieces, but the *Glasgow*, a ship of 4,800 tons, had only two of the 6-inch weapons. It was certain that the German 8-2-inch guns, if the shooting was at all good, would be found to outrange and outclass the British. Cradock was certainly at a disadvantage in gun-power. His protective armour was weaker than that of the enemy.

Nor did his speed give him any superiority. Though the *Glasgow* was capable of twenty-six knots, the flagship and the *Monmouth* could only go to twenty-three. But there was another consideration which the Admiral might weigh. Coming slowly up from the south, but probably still a considerable distance off, was the battleship *Canopus*. Her presence would give the British a decided preponderance. She was a vessel of some 13,000 tons, and her armament included four 12-inch and twelve 6-inch pieces. How far was she away? How soon could she arrive upon the scene? Evening was closing in. Cradock was steering hard in her direction.

If the British, engaging the enemy immediately, could keep them in play throughout the night, when firing must necessarily be desultory, perhaps morning would bring the *Canopus* hastening into the action. It was possible that the Germans did not know of her proximity. They might, accepting the contest, and expecting to cripple the British next morning at their leisure, find themselves trapped. But in any case they should not be allowed to proceed without some such attempt being made to destroy them. It must not be said that, because the enemy was in greater force, a British squadron had taken to flight. Perhaps it would be better, since darkness would afford little opportunity

SIR CHRISTOPHER CRADOCK

of manoeuvring for action, to draw nearer and to engage fairly soon. It was about a quarter past six. The Germans were about 15,000 yards distant. Cradock ordered the speed of his squadron to seventeen knots. He then signalled by wireless to the *Canopus*, 'I am going to attack enemy now'.

The sun was setting. The western horizon was mantled by a canopy of gold. Von Spee's manoeuvre in closing in nearer to the shore had placed him in an advantageous position as regards the light. The British ships, when the sun had set, were sharply outlined against the glowing sky. The Germans were partly hidden in the failing light and by the mountainous coast. The island of Santa Maria, off Coronel, lay in the distance. Von Spee had been gradually closing to within 12,000 yards. The appropriate moment for engaging seemed to be approaching. A few minutes after sunset, about seven o'clock, the leading German cruiser opened fire with her largest guns. Shells shrieked over and short of the *Good Hope*, some falling within five hundred yards.

As battle was now imminent, the *Otranto* began to haul out of line, and to edge away to the south-west. The squadrons were converging rapidly, but the smaller cruisers were as yet out of range. The British replied in quick succession to the German fire. As the distance lessened, each ship engaged that opposite in the line. The *Good Hope* and the *Monmouth* had to bear the brunt of the broadsides of the *Scharnhorst* and the *Gneisenau*. The *Glasgow*, in the rear, exchanged shots with the light cruisers, the *Leipzig* and the *Dresden*. The shooting was deadly. The third of the rapid salvos of the enemy armoured cruisers set the *Good Hope* and the *Monmouth* afire.

Shells began to find their mark, some exploding overhead and bursting in all directions. In about ten minutes the *Monmouth* sheered off the line to westward about one hundred yards. She was being hit heavily. Her foremost turret, shielding one of her 6-inch guns, was in flames. She seemed to be reeling and shaking. She fell back into line, however, and then out again to eastward, her 6-inch guns roaring intermittently. Darkness was now gathering fast. The range had narrowed to about 5,000 yards. The seven ships were all in action.

Many shells striking the sea sent up columns of white spray, showing weirdly in the twilight. It was an impressive scene. The dim light, the heavy seas, the rolling of the vessels, distracted the aim. Some of the guns upon the main decks, being near the water-line, became with each roll almost awash. The British could fire only at the flashes of the enemy's guns. Often the heavy head seas hid even the flashes from the gunlayers. It was impossible to gauge the effect of their shells. The fore-turret of the *Good Hope* burst into flames, and she began to fall away out of line towards the enemy.

The *Glasgow* kept up a continual fire upon the German light cruisers with one of her 6-inch guns and her port batteries. A shell struck her below deck, and men waited for the planks to rise. No explosion nor fire, however, occurred. But the British flagship was now burning brightly forward, and was falling more and more out of line to eastward. It was about a quarter to eight. Suddenly there was the roar of an explosion. The part about the *Good Hope's* after-funnel split asunder, and a column of flame, sparks, and debris was blown up to a height of about two hundred feet. She never fired her guns again. Total destruction must have followed. Sir Christopher Cradock and nine hundred brave sailors went down in the stormy deep. The other ships raced past her in the darkness. The *Monmouth* was in great distress. She left the line after a while, and turned back, steaming with difficulty to north-west. She had ceased firing. The vessels had been travelling at a rate which varied from seven to seventeen knots.

The *Glasgow*, now left alone, eased her speed in order to avoid shells intended for the *Monmouth*. The Germans dropped slowly back. The *Scharnhorst* and the *Gneisenau* now concentrated their salvos upon the *Glasgow*. The range was about 4,500 yards. A shell struck the second funnel: five others hit her side at the waterline, but fortunately not in dangerous places. Luce, her captain, since the flagship was no more, was senior officer. He brought his vessel round and moved rapidly back.

The *Monmouth* had now fallen away to a north-easterly

VICE-ADMIRAL
THE GRAF MAXIMILIAN VON SPEE

course. Luce stood by signalling, Could she steer north-west? She was making water badly forward, Captain Brandt answered, and he wanted to get stem to sea. The enemy were following, Luce signalled again. There was no reply. The *Glasgow* steamed nearer. The *Monmouth* was in a sinking condition. Her bows were under water, and the men were assembled at the stern. The sea was running very high. Rain and mist had come on, though a moon was now rising. The enemy had altered course, and were approaching in line abreast about 6,000 yards away.

A light kept twinkling at regular intervals from one of the ships. They were signalling in Morse, and evidently were forming plans of action. Firing was still proceeding intermittently. It was about half-past eight. Captain Luce could see nothing for it but to abandon the *Monmouth* to her fate. To rescue her crew, under such conditions, was impossible, while to stand by and endeavour to defend her would be folly. The *Glasgow* was not armoured, and could not contend with armoured vessels. Of the two guns she possessed capable of piercing the enemy's armour, one had been put out of action ten minutes after the start. If she stayed and fought to the end, 370 good lives, in addition to the sufficiently heavy toll of 1,600 in the *Good Hope* and the *Monmouth*, would be needlessly sacrificed.

The *Canopus*, moreover, must be warned. She was coming up from the south to sure destruction. She could hardly be expected successfully to combat the whole German squadron. Nevertheless, it must have been with heavy hearts that the men of the *Glasgow* turned away to seek safety in flight. It is recorded that, as they moved off into the darkness, a cheer broke forth from the *Monmouth's* decks. Before the sinking vessel became lost to sight another and a third went up. At about a quarter past nine the *Nürnberg*, which had not been engaged in the main action, came across the *Monmouth*. It is said that, though in a sinking condition, the British ship attempted to ram her enemy. But the *Nürnberg* began to bombard her, and she capsized.

The *Glasgow* steamed off in a north-westerly direction. A few minutes before nine the enemy became lost to sight. Half an hour later many distant flashes of gunfire, the death-struggle of the *Monmouth*, were seen. The play of a searchlight, which lasted a few seconds and then disappeared, was also observed. The vessel bore round gradually to the south. Her wireless was put into operation, and she made efforts to get through to the *Canopus*. But the Germans had again set their apparatus in motion, and the messages were jammed. Only after some hours was the *Glasgow* successful. Steaming hard at twenty-four knots through the heavy seas, her engines and boilers fortunately being intact, she at length joined the battleship. The two ships made straight for the Falkland Islands.

The news of the disaster stirred great alarm in the colony. Before the day on which the ships arrived was out the dismay was further increased. The *Canopus* at first expected to stay ten days. Her presence provided substantial relief. If the enemy appeared, she and even the damaged *Glasgow* could give a very good account of themselves. But during the morning Captain Grant of the *Canopus* received a wireless message from the Admiralty. He was to proceed immediately to Rio de Janeiro with the *Glasgow*. The Brazilian Government had granted the latter permission to enter the dry dock there to make urgent repairs. But seven days only were allowed for this purpose. In the evening the warships cast off, and steamed away to northward.

Stanley was now in an unenviable situation. A powerful German squadron, flushed with victory, was probably making for the Islands. The colony was almost defenceless. All the opposition that the enemy would meet would be from a few hundred volunteers. A wireless message that came through emphasized the imminence of the danger. Warnings and instructions were outlined. If the enemy landed, the volunteers were to fight. But retiring tactics must be adopted. Care should be taken to keep out of range of the enemy's big guns. The Governor at once called a council of war. There could be little doubt that a descent would be made upon the colony.

The position was full of peril. But resistance must certainly be offered. The few women, children, and old men who still remained at Stanley must be sent away immediately. Fortunately the time of year was propitious. November is, indeed, in the Falklands considered the only dry month. The ground is then covered with a variety of sweet-scented flowers. Further, all the stores it was possible to remove must be taken into the 'camp'. Quantities of provisions must be hidden away at various points within reach of the town. In order to add to the mobility of the defending force, it would be well to bring in another hundred horses from the 'camp'. Every man should be mounted. These measures were duly carried out.

Every preparation was made and every precaution taken. Everybody began to pack up boxes of goods. Clothes, stores, and valuables were all taken away to safety. Books, papers, and money were removed from the Government offices, and from the headquarters of the Falkland Islands Company. What was not sent away was buried. The official papers and code-books were buried every night, and dug up and dried every morning. The Governor's tablecloths gave rise to much anxiety. It was thought, since they were marked 'G. R.', they would be liable to insult by the Germans. They were accordingly buried. This conscientious loyalty, however, proved costly. The Governor's silver, wrapped in green baize, was, unfortunately, placed in the same hole. The tablecloths became mixed up with the baize. The damp got through, and the linen was badly stained.

There was a feeling that the attack would come at dawn. People sat up all night, and only went to bed when morning was well advanced. All offices were closed and business was suspended. This state of tension lasted several days. At length, from the look-out post above the town, a warship, apparently a cruiser, was seen making straight for the wireless station. When she got within range she turned broadside on. Her decks were cleared for action. There was a call to arms. Church and dock-yard bells pealed out the alarm. Non-combatants streamed out of the town into the 'camp'. The volunteers paraded, and lined up with their horses. It would soon become a question whether to resist a landing or to retire. In any event the men were ready and provided with emergency rations. But no firing sounded. Signals were exchanged between the vessel and the shore. It was a false alarm. The newcomer was H.M.S. *Canopus*.

She had proceeded, in accordance with her orders, towards Rio de Janeiro with the *Glasgow*. When two days' journey off her destination, however, she received another message. She was directed to return and to defend the Falklands in case of attack. These instructions were received with mingled feelings. To fight alone a powerful squadron was by no means an attractive prospect. Duty, however, was duty. The *Canopus* turned about, and retraced her passage. She set her wireless in operation, and tried to get through to Stanley. But for some reason she was unable to do so. It was concluded that the Germans had made a raid and had destroyed the wireless station. Probably they had occupied the town. The outlook seemed serious. The *Canopus* had her instructions, however, and there was no drawing back. The decks were cleared for action. Ammunition was served out. Guns were loaded and trained. With every man at his post the ship steamed at full speed into the harbour. Great was the relief when it was found that all was well.

The inhabitants were not less relieved. The presence of the battleship was felt to add materially to the security of the town. The Germans would probably hesitate before attacking a ship of her size. If they sustained damage involving loss of fighting efficiency, there was no harbour they could turn to for repair, except so far as their seaworthiness was affected. Nevertheless, it was almost certain that some raid upon the Islands would be attempted. Guns were landed from the ship, and measures were taken to make the defence as effective as possible. Perhaps if the enemy blockaded Stanley, the British would be able to hold out until other warships, certain to be sent to avenge the defeat, arrived. Relief could hardly be expected for two or three weeks.

The Falklands formed a very distant corner of the Empire. It was doubtful, indeed, whether even the ubiquitous German spy had penetrated to these remote and barren shores. It could, however, be recalled that, in 1882, a German expedition had landed on South Georgia, a dependent island of the Falklands, eight hundred miles to their south-east, to observe the transit of Venus.

Upon that same island, indeed, another and a quite unsuspicious expedition had landed, early in that very month, November. Sir Ernest Shackleton, the explorer, had left Buenos Ayres on the morning of October 26, on his way across the Antarctic continent. His little vessel of 230 tons, the *Endurance*, passed through the war zone in safety, and reached South Georgia on November 5. He remained for about a month before leaving for the lonely tracts for which his little party was bound. The island was his last link with civilization. Though sub-Antarctic, it possessed features as up-to-date as electric-light, universal even in pigsties and henhouses. And the march of man, it was observed, had introduced the familiar animals of the farmyard, and even a monkey, into a region whose valleys, destitute of tree or shrub, lay clothed with perpetual snow.

Meanwhile, November passed into December without any appearance of the Germans off the Falklands. The tension became very much relieved. Women and children were brought back to Stanley, after being away a month or six weeks. Messages emanating from the hostile squadron, registered by the wireless station, indicated that the enemy were still in the vicinity. But the condition of the colony became again almost normal. The relief and security were complete when, at length, on Monday, December 7, a powerful British squadron, under Vice-Admiral Sir Doveton Sturdee, arrived at Port Stanley.

There were seven warships, besides the *Canopus*. The *Invincible* and the *Inflexible* had left Plymouth on November 11, and had proceeded to the West Indies. Their mission was to avenge Coronel, They had picked up at Albatross Rock the *Carnarvon*, *Cornwall*, *Bristol*, *Kent*, *Glasgow*, now repaired, and *Macedonia*, an armed liner. All had then steamed southwards towards the Falklands. The vessels started coaling. Officers came ashore to stretch their legs. Certain stores were laid in. It was anticipated that the squadron would depart in search of the enemy on the evening of the following day.

That search might, indeed, be a matter of months. Early next morning, December 8, at about eight o'clock, a volunteer observer posted on Sapper's Hill, two miles from Stanley, sighted two vessels upon the horizon. Twenty minutes later the smoke of two others came into view in the same direction. They were soon recognized as German cruisers. The excitement was intense. The news was immediately carried to the authorities. It was hastily signalled to the fleet. Most of the ships were at anchor in Port William, the outer entrance to Port Stanley. Some of the naval officers were aroused from their repose. It is recorded that, upon hearing the news, the flag-lieutenant dashed down to Admiral Sturdee's cabin, clad in his pyjamas. Sir Doveton was shaving. The lieutenant poured forth his information. 'Well,' said the Admiral, dryly, 'you had better go and get dressed. We'll see about it later.' [1]

The Graf von Spee had, meanwhile, after the Battle of Coronel, been devoting himself to harrying maritime commerce. The Falklands could wait for the present. Since the beginning of hostilities the work of his light cruisers had been moderately successful. The *Nürnberg* had cut the cable between Bamfield, British Columbia, and Fanning Island. The *Leipzig* had accounted for at least four British merchantmen, and the *Dresden* for at least two more. The armed liner *Eitel Friedrich* had also achieved some success. Several traders had had narrow escapes. The Chilian coast was in a state of blockade to British vessels, the ports being crowded with shipping that hesitated to venture forth into the danger zone. The Germans were masters of the Pacific and South Atlantic trade routes.

The Straits of Magellan and the Horn formed a great waterway of commerce, which for sailing vessels was, indeed, the only eastern outlet from the Pacific. But completely as he had the sit-

---

1. The writer cannot vouch for the truth of this anecdote, which he merely records as given in a letter published in the press. But the source from which it was taken, together with many of the preceding details of the condition of Stanley during the period of tension, has proved so accurate in essential points of fact, that their insertion seems justifiable.

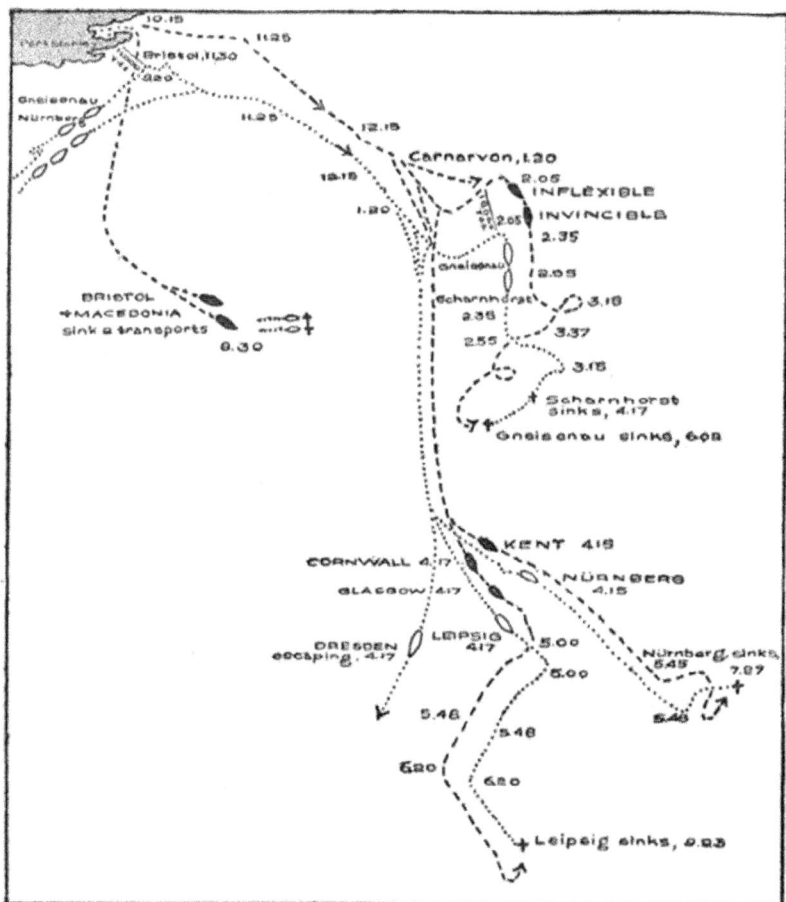

BRITISH AND GERMAN SHIPS AND MOVEMENTS AT THE BATTLE OF
THE FALKLAND ISLANDS, DECEMBER 8, 1914

uation in hand, von Spee was experiencing increasing problems and difficulties with regard to supplies of coal and provisions. Without these he was impotent. He had been employing German merchantmen to great advantage for refueling. But trouble was brewing with the Chilian authorities. Many signs were leading the latter to suspect that, contrary to international law, German traders were loading at Chilian ports cargoes of coal and provisions, contraband of war, and were transferring them at sea to the German warships.

There were other causes of complaint. Juan Fernandez, the isle of romance and of mystery, the home of the original of Robinson Crusoe, was said to have been degraded into use as a base for apportioning the booty, coals and victuals, among the belligerent vessels. The island was a Chilian possession. It was practically certain that von Spee's squadron had stayed there beyond the legal limit of time. A French merchantman had, contrary to rule, also been sunk there by the *Dresden*, within Chilian territorial waters. Inquiries in other quarters were being made, moreover, as to the friendly wireless stations which the Germans had been utilizing secretly in Colombia and Ecuador; while a rumour was current in the United States, that neutral vessels had been seized and pillaged on the high seas. Von Spee soon found that he was nearing the end even of his illegitimate resources. He had tried the patience of the Chilian authorities too far. About the middle of November they suddenly prohibited, as a provisional measure, the vessels of the Kosmos Company from leaving any Chilian port.

On November 24 a Government ship was sent to Juan Fernandez to investigate, and to see that Chilian neutrality was upheld. Many such signs seemed to warn von Spee that the time was appropriate to a sudden disappearance. He gathered his squadron for a descent at last upon the Falklands. His plans must be, not merely for a raid, but for an occupation. There were probably two or three small ships there. They should be sunk. The wireless station must be destroyed. The Islands, after a landing had been effected and the defence reduced, could be used as a base for the German operations.

There were large quantities of coal and stores at Stanley. The harbour possessed facilities for refitting. To dislodge a strong German naval force, with adequate guns, placed in occupation of the colony, would be a difficult task for the enemy. The Falklands had many possibilities. According to von Spee's information they were feebly defended and would fall an easy prey. At length, early in the morning of December 8. the Admiral brought his fleet off Stanley. His five cruisers approached from the south. They were, of course, observed. A warning gun, probably from one of the small ships which he would shortly sink, sounded the alarm inside the harbour.

There was no need, however, for haste At twenty minutes past nine the *Gneisenau* and the *Nürnberg* moved towards the wireless station, and brought their guns to bear upon it. But suddenly from inside the harbour there came the thunder of a big gun. Five shells, of very heavy calibre, screamed in quick succession from over the low-lying land. One of the vessels was struck. Surprise and bewilderment took the Germans, This was most unexpected. The *Gneisenau* and the *Nürnberg* hastily retired out of range.

Sir Doveton and his fleet, meanwhile, had gone to breakfast. Steam for full speed was got up as rapidly as possible. Coaling operations had recommenced at 6.30 that morning. The colliers were hurriedly cast off, and the decks were cleared for action. Officers and men were delighted at the prospect of an early fight. The Germans had saved them a long cold search around the Horn by calling for them. There was going to be no mistake this time. The enemy could not escape. Sturdee's squadron was superior both in weight and speed to the German. It consisted of two battle-cruisers of over 17,000 tons, the *Invincible* and *Inflexible*; of three cruisers of about 10,000 tons, the *Carnarvon*, *Kent*, and *Cornwall*; and of two light cruisers of 4,800 tons, the *Glasgow* and *Bristol*.

The primary armament of the *Invincible* and *Inflexible* was eight 12-inch guns; of the *Carnarvon*, four 7-5-inch; of the *Kent* and *Cornwall*, fourteen 6-inch; of the *Glasgow* and *Bristol*, two 6-inch. The speed of the battle-cruisers was twenty-eight knots; of the three middle-class cruisers, twenty-two to twenty-four knots; and of the light cruisers, twenty-five to twenty-six knots. In size, in armament, in speed, the British squadron would decidedly preponderate. Admiral Sturdee, however, though confident of victory, was determined to take no risks, and to minimize loss in men and material by making full use of his superior long-range gunfire, and of his superior speed. He would wait, screened by the land, until the Germans had drawn nearer.

Everything should be got ready carefully. Undue excitement was to be deprecated. Meanwhile, he watched the enemy closely. At about a quarter to nine, Captain Grant of the *Canopus* reported that the first two ships sighted were now about eight miles away: the other two were still at a distance of some twenty miles. The *Kent* passed down the harbour and took up a position at the entrance. Five minutes later the smoke of a fifth German vessel was observed. When, in about half an hour's time, the two leading enemy ships made a threatening move in the direction of the wireless station, the Admiral ordered a swift counterstroke. Officers upon the hills above the town signalled the range, 11,000 yards, to the *Canopus*. She opened fire with her 12-inch guns.

The Germans hoisted their colours and drew back. Their masts and smoke were now visible from the upper bridge of the *Invincible* across the low land bounding Port William on the south. Within a few minutes the two cruisers altered course and made for the harbour-mouth. Here the *Kent* lay stationed. It seemed that the Germans were about to engage her. As, however, they approached, the masts and funnels of two large ships at anchor within the port became visible to them. The *Gneisenau* and the *Nürnberg* could hardly expect to contend alone with this force. They at once changed their direction, and moved back at increased speed to join their consorts.

The morning was gloriously fine. The sun shone brightly, the sky was clear, the sea was calm, and a breeze blew lightly from the north-west. It was one of the rare bright stretches that visit the Islands, for usually rain falls, mostly in misty drizzles, on about 250 days in the year. At twenty minutes to ten the *Glasgow* weighed anchor, and joined the *Kent* at the harbour-mouth. Five minutes later the rest of the squadron weighed, and began to steam out.

The battleship *Canopus*, her speed making her unsuitable for a chase, was left in harbour. The *Bristol* and the *Macedonia* also remained behind for the present. By a dexterous use of oil fuel the two battle-cruisers were kept shrouded as much as possible in dense clouds of smoke. The enemy for some time could not gauge their size. But as vessel after vessel emerged, Admiral von Spee grew uneasy. The English were in altogether unexpected strength. His squadron could not cope with such force. He had played into the enemy's hands, and unless he could outspeed their ships, the game was up. Without hesitation, he steamed off at high speed to eastward.

The British followed, steaming at fifteen to eighteen knots. The enemy, to their south-east, were easily visible. At twenty past ten an order for a general chase was signalled. The *Invincible* and the *Inflexible* quickly drew to the fore. The Germans were roughly in line abreast, 20,000 yards, or some eleven miles, ahead. The morning sunlight, the gleaming seas, the grey warships, white foam springing from their bows, tearing at high speed through the waves, formed a magnificent spectacle. Crowds of the inhabitants of Stanley gathered upon the hills above the town to view the chase. The excitement and enthusiasm were intense. The vessels were in sight about two hours.

At about a quarter past eleven it was reported from a point in the south of East Falkland that three other German ships were in sight. They were probably colliers or transports. The *Bristol* signalled the information to Admiral Sturdee. He at once ordered her, with the armed liner *Macedonia*, to hasten in their direction and destroy them. The newcomers made off to south-west, and the British followed. Meanwhile, the rest of the squadron, now travelling at twenty-three knots, Mere slowly closing upon the enemy. The distance had narrowed to 15-16,000 yards. The British were within striking range. Nevertheless, Sturdee decided to wait till after dinner before engaging. His guns could outdistance those of the enemy. It would be advisable for him to keep at long range.

The Germans, on the other hand, would be forced, when firing commenced, to alter course and draw in, in order to bring their own guns into play. The men had their midday meal at twelve o'clock as usual. It is said that comfortable time was allowed afterwards for a smoke. The *Invincible, Inflexible*, and *Glasgow* at about 12.30. increased their speed to between twenty-five and twenty-eight knots, and went on ahead. Just after a quarter to one there was a signal from the Admiral: 'Open fire and engage the enemy.' A few minutes later there were sharp commands. The ranges were signalled, and the bigger guns were laid. Fiery glares and dense clouds of smoke burst suddenly from their muzzles. The air quivered with their thunder. Shells went screaming in the direction of the nearest light cruiser, the *Leipzig*, which was dropping rapidly astern.

The firing was uncomfortably accurate. The three smaller German cruisers very soon left the line, and made an attempt, veering off to the south, to scatter and escape. Flame and smoke issued from the Leipzig, before she drew clear, where a shell had struck. Sir Doveton Sturdee directed the *Glasgow, Kent*, and *Cornwall* to pursue the German light cruisers. With his remaining vessels, the *Invincible*, the *Inflexible*, and the slower *Carnarvon*, he turned upon the *Scharnhorst* and the *Gneisenau*, and began operations in earnest.

The interval of sunlight which had opened the day with such promise was of short duration. The sky became overcast. Soon after four o'clock the air was thick with rain-mist. From 1.15 onwards for three hours a fierce duel was maintained between the two British battle-cruisers and the two German armoured cruisers. The enemy made every effort to get away. They replied to the British fire for some time, having dropped back to within 13,500 yards. But shortly after two o'clock they changed their course, and began to haul out to south-east. The *Invincible* and the *Inflexible* had eased their speed, and the range now widened by about 3,000 yards.

A second chase ensued. A full-rigged sailing-ship appeared in the distance at about a quarter to three. Her crew must have beheld an awe-inspiring scene. Shortly before the hour firing recommenced. The action began to develop. Great coolness and efficiency were shown on board the British vessels. Every man was at his battle-station, behind armour. Fire-control parties were at their instruments. Water from numerous hoses was flooding the decks as a precaution against fire. The roaring of the discharges, the screaming of the shells, the clangour of metal upon metal, the crashes of the explosions, made up a tumult that was painful in its intensity.

During intervals in the firing came the rushing of the waves and of the breeze, and the grinding and grunting of the hydraulic engines in the turrets, where swung, training constantly upon the enemy, the greater guns. The Germans soon began to show signs of distress. The *Scharnhorst* particularly suffered. Dense clouds of smoke, making it difficult for the British accurately to gauge the damage, rose from her decks. Shells rending her side disclosed momentarily the dull red glow of flame. She was burning fiercely. The firing on both sides was deadly, though the German had slackened considerably. But the British vessels, through their preponderance in gunfire, suffered little damage. Their 12-inch guns hit their marks constantly, while the 8.2-inch guns of the *Scharnhorst* were accurate, but ineffective. She veered to starboard at about 3.30, to bring into play her starboard batteries. Both her masts and three of her four funnels were shot away.

At length the German flagship began to settle down rapidly in the waters. It was about a quarter past four. There was a swirl of the seas and a rush of steam and smoke. The *Scharnhorst* disappeared. She went down with her flag flying to an ocean grave, bearing 760 brave men and a gallant admiral, whose name will deservedly rank high in the annals of German naval history. The

Gneisenau passed on the far side of her sunken flag-ship. With the guns of both battle-cruisers now bearing upon her alone, the German was soon in sore straits. But she fought on gallantly for a considerable time.

At half-past five she had ceased firing, and appeared to be sinking. She had suffered severe damage. Smoke and steam were rising everywhere. Her bridge had been shot away. Her foremost funnel was resting against the second. Her upper deck was so shattered that it could not be crossed, and every man upon it had been killed. An exploding shell had hurled one of the gun-turrets bodily overboard. Fire was raging aft. Her colours had been shot away several times, and hoisted as often. One of the flags was hauled down at about twenty to six, though that at the peak was still flying. She began to fire again with a single gun. The *Invincible*, the *Inflexible*, and the *Carnarvon*, which had now come up, closed in upon the doomed vessel. Firing was recommenced.

The *Gneisenau* was not moving. Both her engines were smashed. Shells striking the water near her sent up colossal columns of water, which, falling upon the ship, put out some of the fires. She soon began to settle down in the waves. All her guns were now out of action, and Sturdee ordered the 'Cease fire'. There could be little doubt that her stubborn resistance was nearing its end. The German commander lined up his men on the decks. The ammunition was exhausted. The ship would soon go down. Some six hundred men had already been killed. The survivors had better provide themselves with articles for their support in the water.

At six o'clock the *Gneisenau* heeled over suddenly. Clouds of steam sprang forth. Her stem swung up into the air, and she sank. Large numbers of her crew could be seen floating in the icy waves, hanging on to pieces of wreckage, and uttering terribly uncanny cries. The sea was choppy. Drizzling rain was falling. The British steamed up immediately. All undamaged boats were got out. Ropes were lowered. Lifebuoys and spars were thrown to the drowning men. But many of them, numbed by the freezing water, let go their hold and sank. About 180, among them the captain of the *Gneisenau*, were saved. It is said that much agreeable surprise, upon the discovery that their anticipations of being shot would not be realized, was manifested by the German sailors.

Meanwhile, battle had been in progress elsewhere. The *Bristol* and the *Macedonia* had overtaken the transports *Baden* and *Santa Isabel*, had captured their crews, and had sunk the ships. The armed liner accompanying them, the *Eitel Friedrich*, had, however, made off and got away by means of her superior speed. The *Kent*, *Glasgow*, and *Cornwall* had pursued the German light cruisers in a southerly direction. The *Dresden*, the fastest, proved too speedy a vessel to overtake. She was ahead of her consorts, upon either quarter, and made her escape whilst they were being engaged. The *Kent* gave chase to the *Nürnberg*. The *Glasgow*, in pursuit of the *Leipzig*, raced ahead of the *Cornwall*, and by about three o'clock in the afternoon had closed sufficiently, within 12,000 yards, to open fire with her foremost guns. The German ship turned every now and then to fire a salvo. Soon a regular battle began which was maintained for some hours. Shells fell all around the *Glasgow*.

There were several narrow escapes, but the casualties were few. Shortly after six a wireless message was received from Admiral Sturdee, announcing that the *Scharnhorst* and the *Gneisenau* had been sunk. A cheer surged up, and the men set to work with renewed spirits and energy. The *Cornwall* had come up some time before, and the *Leipzig* was now severely damaged. But she fought on for three more hours. Darkness came on. The German cruiser began to burn fore and aft. It was nine o'clock before she at last turned over and sank.

The British vessels had, during the course of the action, steamed miles apart, and far out of sight of land. During the evening and night they began to get into touch with one another and with Stanley by means of their wireless. All the ships except the *Kent* were accounted for, and reported all well. But no reply was forthcoming to the numerous calls, 'Kent, Kent,

Kent', that were sent out. She had, in chase of the *Nürnberg*, lost all touch with the rest of the squadron. There was great uneasiness. It was feared that she had been lost. The other ships were directed to search for her, and for the *Nürnberg* and the *Dresden*. Late in the afternoon of the following day, however, she entered Stanley harbour safely. Her wireless had been destroyed, but she had sunk the *Nürnberg*, after a very stern struggle.

The German captain, Schönberg, is reported, indeed, to have said at Honolulu, 'The *Nürnberg* will very likely be our coffin. But we are ready to fight to the last'. He had fought and died true to his words. The German ship was ordinarily more than a knot faster than the British. But the engineers and stokers of the *Kent* rose magnificently to the occasion. Fuel was piled high. Her engines were strained to the. utmost. Soon she was speeding through the waves at twenty-five knots, a knot and a half more than her registered speed. The *Nürnberg* drew nearer. At five o'clock she was within range, and firing was opened. A sharp action began which lasted some two and a half hours.

The *Kent* was struck many times, and lost several men. She had one narrow escape. A bursting shell ignited some cordite charges, and a flash of flame went down the hoist into the ammunition passage. Some empty shell bags began to burn. But a sergeant picked up a cordite charge and hurled it out of danger. Seizing a fire hose, he flooded the compartment and extinguished the fire. A disastrous explosion, which might have proved fatal to the vessel, was thus averted. Her silken ensign and jack, presented by the ladies of *Kent*, were torn to ribbons. The gallant captain collected the pieces, some being caught in the rigging, and carefully preserved them. The *Nürnberg*, however, was soon in sore straits. Many shells struck her, and she was set afire.

Day drew into evening, and darkness deepened. The Germans ceased firing, and the *Kent*, within about 3,000 yards, followed suit upon the enemy's colours being hauled down. The *Nürnberg* sank just before half-past seven. As she disappeared beneath the surface, men upon her quarter-deck were waving the German ensign. The *Kent*, after picking up some survivors, put about, and returned to Stanley.

Here the rest of the squadron soon gathered. Congratulatory telegrams began to pour in to Sir Doveton Sturdee. And the curtain closed, in the flush of triumph, upon the most memorable and most dramatic episode in the history of the Falklands.

One further episode remains to complete the story. The *Dresden* and the armed liner *Eitel Friedrich*, the sole survivors of the German squadron, made once more for the Pacific. They were lost sight of for many weeks. Suspicious movements and activities on the part of German merchantmen were, however, again observed. The Government wireless station at Valparaiso intercepted messages from the Dresden summoning friendly vessels to bring her supplies. Persistent rumours began to be circulated that she was hiding in the inlets of southern Chili.

During January, 1915, the *Eitel Friedrich* seized and destroyed six vessels, chiefly sailing-ships, some in Pacific, most in Atlantic waters. In February she accounted for four more. Towards the end of the month a British *barque* was sunk by the *Dresden*. The position was again rapidly becoming troublesome. The movement of British shipping on the Chilian coast had to be suspended. But the *Glasgow* and the *Kent* were on the *Dresden's* track. The *Kent* entered Coronel on March 13, coaled, and departed the same night.

The *Eitel Friedrich*, meanwhile, had arrived at Newport News, a United States port, with her engines badly in need of repair. Much indignation was aroused among Americans by the announcement that one of her victims had been an American vessel. The German liner had many prisoners on board Declarations of a resolve, if he had been caught by the British, to have sunk fighting to the last, were repeatedly and emphatically declaimed by the German captain. Five days later he learned that the *Dresden* had tamely surrendered off Juan Fernandez after a five minutes' action.

The *Kent*, at nine o'clock on the morning after she had left Coronel, together with the *Glasgow* and the auxiliary cruiser

Orama, came up with the *Dresden* near the island. A sharp en-counter followed. The German cruiser was hit heavily. Fire broke out. In five minutes' time she hauled down her colours and hoisted a white flag. The crew were taken off. The *Dresden* continued to burn for some time, until finally her magazine exploded and she sank. The German officers contended that their vessel was sunk within Chilian territorial waters.

It had not hitherto been noticeable that their consciences were concerned to maintain Chilian neutrality inviolate. The Battle of the Falkland Islands was the first decisive naval contest of the war. It removed a formidable menace to the trade routes. It relieved British convoys and transports from danger of interruption. It freed many battleships and cruisers, engaged in sweeping the oceans, for other usefulness. It gave Great Britain effective mastery of the outer seas. Henceforth German naval ambition, frustrated in its endeavour to disorganize the trade routes, was forced, within the limits of the North Sea and of British waters, to seek less adventurous but more disreputable ends.

A series of bombardments of coast towns was planned. A preliminary success was followed by a galling disaster. Foiled a second time, Germany is attempting now, (at time of first publication), to terrorize British waters, by deliberate submarine piracy, to all maritime commerce. Her project has elicited the protests of neutral States. It has excited no dismay among the allied nations.

LEONAUR

ALSO FROM LEONAUR
AVAILABLE IN SOFTCOVER OR HARDCOVER WITH DUST JACKET

AT THEM WITH THE BAYONET *by Donald F. Featherstone*—The first Anglo-Sikh War 1845-1846.

STEPHEN CRANE'S BATTLES *by Stephen Crane*—Nine Decisive Battles Recounted by the Author of 'The Red Badge of Courage'.

THE GURKHA WAR *by H. T. Prinsep*—The Anglo-Nepalese Conflict in North East India 1814-1816.

FIRE & BLOOD *by G. R. Gleig*—The burning of Washington & the battle of New Orleans, 1814, through the eyes of a young British soldier.

SOUND ADVANCE! *by Joseph Anderson*—Experiences of an officer of HM 50th regiment in Australia, Burma & the Gwalior war.

THE CAMPAIGN OF THE INDUS *by Thomas Holdsworth*—Experiences of a British Officer of the 2nd (Queen's Royal) Regiment in the Campaign to Place Shah Shuja on the Throne of Afghanistan 1838 - 1840.

WITH THE MADRAS EUROPEAN REGIMENT IN BURMA *by John Butler*—The Experiences of an Officer of the Honourable East India Company's Army During the First Anglo-Burmese War 1824 - 1826.

IN ZULULAND WITH THE BRITISH ARMY *by Charles L. Norris-Newman*—The Anglo-Zulu war of 1879 through the first-hand experiences of a special correspondent.

BESIEGED IN LUCKNOW *by Martin Richard Gubbins*—The first Anglo-Sikh War 1845-1846.

A TIGER ON HORSEBACK *by L. March Phillips*—The Experiences of a Trooper & Officer of Rimington's Guides - The Tigers - during the Anglo-Boer war 1899 - 1902.

SEPOYS, SIEGE & STORM *by Charles John Griffiths*—The Experiences of a young officer of H.M.'s 61st Regiment at Ferozepore, Delhi ridge and at the fall of Delhi during the Indian mutiny 1857.

CAMPAIGNING IN ZULULAND *by W. E. Montague*—Experiences on campaign during the Zulu war of 1879 with the 94th Regiment.

THE STORY OF THE GUIDES *by G.J. Younghusband*—The Exploits of the Soldiers of the famous Indian Army Regiment from the northwest frontier 1847 - 1900.

LEONAUR

ALSO FROM LEONAUR
AVAILABLE IN SOFTCOVER OR HARDCOVER WITH DUST JACKET

OFFICERS & GENTLEMEN *by Peter Hawker & William Graham*—Two Accounts of British Officers During the Peninsula War: Officer of Light Dragoons by Peter Hawker & Campaign in Portugal and Spain by William Graham .

THE WALCHEREN EXPEDITION *by Anonymous*—The Experiences of a British Officer of the 81st Regt. During the Campaign in the Low Countries of 1809.

LADIES OF WATERLOO *by Charlotte A. Eaton, Magdalene de Lancey & Juana Smith*—The Experiences of Three Women During the Campaign of 1815: Waterloo Days by Charlotte A. Eaton, A Week at Waterloo by Magdalene de Lancey & Juana's Story by Juana Smith.

JOURNAL OF AN OFFICER IN THE KING'S GERMAN LEGION *by John Frederick Hering*—Recollections of Campaigning During the Napoleonic Wars.

JOURNAL OF AN ARMY SURGEON IN THE PENINSULAR WAR *by Charles Boutflower*—The Recollections of a British Army Medical Man on Campaign During the Napoleonic Wars.

ON CAMPAIGN WITH MOORE AND WELLINGTON *by Anthony Hamilton*—The Experiences of a Soldier of the 43rd Regiment During the Peninsular War.

THE ROAD TO AUSTERLITZ *by R. G. Burton*—Napoleon's Campaign of 1805.

SOLDIERS OF NAPOLEON *by A. J. Doisy De Villargennes & Arthur Chuquet*—The Experiences of the Men of the French First Empire: Under the Eagles by A. J. Doisy De Villargennes & Voices of 1812 by Arthur Chuquet .

INVASION OF FRANCE, 1814 *by F. W. O. Maycock*—The Final Battles of the Napoleonic First Empire.

LEIPZIG—A CONFLICT OF TITANS *by Frederic Shoberl*—A Personal Experience of the 'Battle of the Nations' During the Napoleonic Wars, October 14th-19th, 1813.

SLASHERS *by Charles Cadell*—The Campaigns of the 28th Regiment of Foot During the Napoleonic Wars by a Serving Officer.

BATTLE IMPERIAL *by Charles William Vane*—The Campaigns in Germany & France for the Defeat of Napoleon 1813-1814.

SWIFT & BOLD *by Gibbes Rigaud*—The 60th Rifles During the Peninsula War.

LEONAUR

ALSO FROM LEONAUR
AVAILABLE IN SOFTCOVER OR HARDCOVER WITH DUST JACKET

THE LIFE OF THE REAL BRIGADIER GERARD VOLUME 1—THE YOUNG HUSSAR 1782-1807 *by Jean-Baptiste De Marbot*—A French Cavalryman Of the Napoleonic Wars at Marengo, Austerlitz, Jena, Eylau & Friedland.

THE LIFE OF THE REAL BRIGADIER GERARD VOLUME 2—IMPERIAL AIDE-DE-CAMP 1807-1811 *by Jean-Baptiste De Marbot*—A French Cavalryman of the Napoleonic Wars at Saragossa, Landshut, Eckmuhl, Ratisbon, Aspern-Essling, Wagram, Busaco & Torres Vedras.

THE LIFE OF THE REAL BRIGADIER GERARD VOLUME 3—COLONEL OF CHASSEURS 1811-1815 *by Jean-Baptiste De Marbot*—A French Cavalryman in the retreat from Moscow, Lutzen, Bautzen, Katzbach, Leipzig, Hanau & Waterloo.

THE INDIAN WAR OF 1864 *by Eugene Ware*—The Experiences of a Young Officer of the 7th Iowa Cavalry on the Western Frontier During the Civil War.

THE MARCH OF DESTINY *by Charles E. Young & V. Devinny*—Dangers of the Trail in 1865 by Charles E. Young & The Story of a Pioneer by V. Devinny, two Accounts of Early Emigrants to Colorado.

CROSSING THE PLAINS *by William Audley Maxwell*—A First Hand Narrative of the Early Pioneer Trail to California in 1857.

CHIEF OF SCOUTS *by William F. Drannan*—A Pilot to Emigrant and Government Trains, Across the Plains of the Western Frontier.

THIRTY-ONE YEARS ON THE PLAINS AND IN THE MOUNTAINS *by William F. Drannan*—William Drannan was born to be a pioneer, hunter, trapper and wagon train guide during the momentous days of the Great American West.

THE INDIAN WARS VOLUNTEER *by William Thompson*—Recollections of the Conflict Against the Snakes, Shoshone, Bannocks, Modocs and Other Native Tribes of the American North West.

THE 4TH TENNESSEE CAVALRY *by George B. Guild*—The Services of Smith's Regiment of Confederate Cavalry by One of its Officers.

COLONEL WORTHINGTON'S SHILOH *by T. Worthington*—The Tennessee Campaign, 1862, by an Officer of the Ohio Volunteers.

FOUR YEARS IN THE SADDLE *by W. L. Curry*—The History of the First Regiment Ohio Volunteer Cavalry in the American Civil War.

LEONAUR

ALSO FROM LEONAUR

AVAILABLE IN SOFTCOVER OR HARDCOVER WITH DUST JACKET

ESCAPE FROM THE FRENCH *by Edward Boys*—A Young Royal Navy Midshipman's Adventures During the Napoleonic War.

THE VOYAGE OF H.M.S. PANDORA *by Edward Edwards R. N. & George Hamilton, edited by Basil Thomson*—In Pursuit of the Mutineers of the Bounty in the South Seas—1790-1791.

MEDUSA *by J. B. Henry Savigny and Alexander Correard and Charlotte-Adélaïde Dard* —Narrative of a Voyage to Senegal in 1816 & The Sufferings of the Picard Family After the Shipwreck of the Medusa.

THE SEA WAR OF 1812 VOLUME 1 *by A. T. Mahan*—A History of the Maritime Conflict.

THE SEA WAR OF 1812 VOLUME 2 *by A. T. Mahan*—A History of the Maritime Conflict.

WETHERELL OF H. M. S. HUSSAR *by John Wetherell*—The Recollections of an Ordinary Seaman of the Royal Navy During the Napoleonic Wars.

THE NAVAL BRIGADE IN NATAL *by C. R. N. Burne*—With the Guns of H. M. S. Terrible & H. M. S. Tartar during the Boer War 1899-1900.

THE VOYAGE OF H. M. S. BOUNTY *by William Bligh*—The True Story of an 18th Century Voyage of Exploration and Mutiny.

SHIPWRECK! *by William Gilly*—The Royal Navy's Disasters at Sea 1793-1849.

KING'S CUTTERS AND SMUGGLERS: 1700-1855 *by E. Keble Chatterton*—A unique period of maritime history-from the beginning of the eighteenth to the middle of the nineteenth century when British seamen risked all to smuggle valuable goods from wool to tea and spirits from and to the Continent.

CONFEDERATE BLOCKADE RUNNER *by John Wilkinson*—The Personal Recollections of an Officer of the Confederate Navy.

NAVAL BATTLES OF THE NAPOLEONIC WARS *by W. H. Fitchett*—Cape St.Vincent, the Nile, Cadiz, Copenhagen, Trafalgar & Others.

PRISONERS OF THE RED DESERT *by R. S. Gwatkin-Williams*—The Adventures of the Crew of the Tara During the First World War.

U-BOAT WAR 1914-1918 *by James B. Connolly/Karl von Schenk*—Two Contrasting Accounts from Both Sides of the Conflict at Sea D uring the Great War.

www.ingramcontent.com/pod-product-compliance
Lightning Source LLC
Chambersburg PA
CBHW032017090426
42741CB00006B/627